Strike a Rock

Strike a Rock
The Thembi Kgatlana Story

Nikolaos Kirkinis

Email: nikolaosmichaelkirkinis@gmail.com
Instagram: @niko_kirkinis

First published by Jacana Media (Pty) Ltd in 2021

10 Orange Street
Sunnyside
Auckland Park 2092
South Africa
+2711 628 3200
www.jacana.co.za

© Nikolaos Kirkinis, 2021

All rights reserved.

ISBN 978-1-4314-3133-5

Cover design by publicide
Editing by Joey Kok
Proofreading by Nkhensani Manabe
Set in Sabon 11/15pt
Printed and bound by ABC Press, Cape Town
Job no. 003801

See a complete list of Jacana titles at www.jacana.co.za

Contents

Acronyms and Abbreviations......................vii

1. Greatness..1
2. 1996..3
3. This Cake Isn't for Children.........................7
4. Boys and Girls....................................10
5. Cruel Bathrooms..................................16
6. The Trouble Twins................................22
7. Cops Come Visit..................................30
8. They Pay Her?....................................33
9. A Thug in the House..............................37
10. Toughening Up...................................42
11. Can't Come Home................................47
12. Crazier than Usual...............................50
13. Injure One, Injure All............................52
14. The Biggest Bag We Have........................57
15. Step Up or Step Out..............................60

16. Books and Boots 66
17. Not Good Enough 71
18. Portia Has Left the Building 79
19. Operation Rio de Janeiro 81
20. Are You Even a Part of This Team? 89
21. Changing Momentum 93
22. A Whack Left Foot 96
23. What Is the Purpose of Your Visit to America? 101
24. Save the Brother 109
25. I Thought You Were Better 114
26. What Do You Want From Paris? 117
27. A Starry Night in Senegal 125
28. Homecoming 135
29. Royalty 138
30. Dogs in the East 142
31. Dutch Doctors 147
32. The Jamaica Incident 151
33. This House Is Haunted 155
34. My Success Is Our Success 157
35. The Eagles of Portugal 163
36. I Tell My Daughter About You 176
37. Fearless in France 180

ACRONYMS AND ABBREVIATIONS

AWCON	Africa Women's Cup of Nations
CAF	Confederation of African Football
COSAFA	Council of Southern African Football Associations
HPC	High Performance Centre at the University of Pretoria, training camp for Banyana Banyana
SAFA	South African Football Association
TUT	Tshwane University of Technology
UEFA	Union of European Football Associations
UWC	University of the Western Cape

CHAPTER 1
Greatness

She should not be here. The girl child from a South African township should not be here. Ears rattling, legs shaking, heart pulsing, she should not be here. The air is different over here. It stings the nostrils with spices of success, opportunity and potential. Thembi is a long way from home. The stadium feels like a living beast, roaring out of its stands, breathing through its tunnels and beating its heart from the field. Before Thembi waits the biggest moment of her life, behind her sits very little opportunity at all. A South African flag wraps itself around her arm, the brave colours of red, green, white, black, blue and gold. Each representing an aspect of the struggle that came before Thembi could stand here today. The flag pressed to her arm reminds Thembi that she does not just represent herself today, and the feeling in her chest tells her that this is much more than a game. You see, Thembi's story is not just a story about football. This is a story about life. This is a story about struggle. This story will take you into the township and sit you down in the back of police vans. This story will put you face to face with drug addiction. This story will take you around the world, it will walk you down streets in China, have you in interrogation rooms in America and soaring with eagles in Portugal. This story is about much more than football. This story is an African story. This story is woven with bold threads – comedy, action and tragedy, this is a South

African story. This story is not just about Thembi Kgatlana. This is the story of an incredible class of South African women who went on to achieve what no one had before. This is the story of the dream-carriers, the women who keep the hopes of others alive on their shoulders. This story will take you many places, but it all begins in the year 1996, somewhere in the heart of Mohlakeng...

CHAPTER 2
1996

1996 promises to be an electric year for South Africa. The wrath of apartheid has officially died, but practically its mark is still left in every corner and under every stone in the country. Many places do not look too different now from what they did before the first democratic election two years ago. One such unchanging place is Mohlakeng, a township on the fringes of Johannesburg's West Rand.

Mohlakeng is a tough place. A place of bricks, dust and gravel. Unbearably hot in the summer and twice as cold in the winter. Some notable names have graduated from this location: Oupa Manyisa, Ace Khuse and Ace Ntsoelengoe – some of the greatest footballers of all time – and of course Terror Mathebula, a world champion boxer. All of them began in the gravel and the dust though. It is not a particularly large township. It was set up in 1954, the people who originally lived here found themselves displaced from nearby Randfontein where human life had to be cleared to make way for a factory.

In 1996 though, Mohlakeng, much like many football-loving locations across the country, is in a state of joy. Two massive events happen around the middle of the year that will have an impact on the future of the sport in the country.

It's 3 February. Soweto is alive. It is the final of the 1996 African Cup of Nations. The hope that bounces off one citizen's shoulders onto the next is electric, tangible. It is a good time to be a South African. A new country is in the works. As 100 000 people descend on FNB Stadium and its iconic turquoise seats, there is a sense that this game carries more significance than others. South Africa has an opportunity to introduce itself to the world. The problem is, South Africa does not exist yet. It is just a concept, a promise of what a country could be. Today, the new state will go toe to toe with Tunisia. A giant in its own regard. It would be easy to see this as just another cup final, but it would not be accurate. South Africa may have been born four years earlier, but tonight she takes her first steps. When Bafana Bafana wins the game 2-0, it is a promise to the nation. A promise that greatness is within our grasp, and from unlikely odds we will fight our way to glory.

As Nelson Mandela hands captain Neil Tovey the trophy, somewhere in Mohlakeng, a heavily pregnant Constance Masinga is on her feet. Her hands are in the air, and the smile has not dissolved from her lips since Mark Williams put that second goal in the back of the net. A man's hand reaches up and grabs hers in the air. She looks at the hand and then down at the man. It is Matlhomola Kgatlana and he is smiling too. They had met not too long ago, at a well-known house on Mohapi Street, number 70. Constance's mother sells umqombothi out of their house, and Constance has recently been taught by her mother how to brew the traditional beer by mixing bread, yeast, called umthombo, and sugar. The whole process takes a few days. Matlhomola is a regular customer at the house; he has been for a while. He took a fancy to Constance instantly and stays for longer on the nights she is working.

In the house, it is not uncommon for drama to follow the alcohol. Men often argue intensely, and sometimes physically. Matlhomola always puts his beer down immediately, springs to his feet and separates the fighting men, telling them to settle their quarrel outside. He always checks to make sure Constance is watching. Constance thinks little of the man at first, but her sister approaches her one day with an idea: "Who is that man? The one who is always walking up and down Mohapi Street buying things?

He must be a very rich man. We should see if he can buy us some alcohol too."

After sharing a few drinks on a number of occasions, Matlhomola asks Constance to be his girlfriend. She is thrilled, but her mother is not. Her mother's greatest cause for concern is the fact that the man is nine years older than her daughter. She even goes so far as to call Matlhomola a rapist and to tell him that he should be ashamed of himself for dating such a young girl. However, soon, she has to let go of the fight and accept Matlhomola as a part of the family's life. Constance is now pregnant, and as much as her mother hates her dating an older man, she hates the idea of Constance being a single mother even more. She allows Matlhomola into her house. For in three months, her daughter will be giving birth to Chrestinah Thembi Kgatlana.

By the time Thembi is born in Leratong Hospital on 2 May 1996, there are already two children living at home. Tumelo Masinga is Constance's firstborn, but he is not Matlhomola's child. Mpho Masinga is Thembi's cousin, but you can also refer to him as her brother. He was born just the year before her. Mpho and Thembi are inseparable from an early age. Whether walking to the shops or kicking a stone on the way home from school, Thembi and Mpho are always seen together.

The family moves around Mohlakeng often. At the dawn of democracy, the new government implements a programme called RDP. Among many other things, it involves building simple houses for low-income families. It is far from a perfect system, there is a long waiting list just to get allocated a house, and many aspects of the whole process are captured by opportunists. However, the Kgatlana family is one that does get afforded an RDP house. Thembi is too young to appreciate the programme, but she is not too young to notice that the tap trickles no water and the light bulb flickers no electricity. There may be a roof over their heads, but, other than that, it barely resembles a house. This is no place for a family to live.

Jobs are not easy to come by in South Africa. Matlhomola has recently been retrenched from his work. Luckily, Constance finds a cleaning job at a nearby private clinic. It is at this point that the family is forced to split, temporarily. Thembi, her mom and dad stay in a backroom in Thembi's aunt's house. At the same time, Thembi's brothers Tumelo and Mpho stay with their grandmother in Mohapi Street. It is a rare moment in township life, where Thembi and her parents get a space to themselves. It is no luxury, but it is private.

The situation is not like this for too long. One evening, the wind comes calling for Thembi's grandmother, and she passes on from this life. One of the results of this tragedy is that Thembi and her parents move into the house on Mohapi Street. Technically it belongs to neither of them. However, they know that they have grandmother's blessing from above to live there.

CHAPTER 3

This Cake Isn't for Children

Thembi and Mpho wake up in their shared room. This is early 2002. They're excited. Usually, they are both deep sleepers, but today they are awake before the rooster. They speak about animals: giraffes, elephants, tigers and rhinos. Mpho asks Thembi who would win in a fight between a shark and a crocodile, Thembi asks who would win in a race between a leopard and a lion. The reason for their animal enthusiasm is because the school is taking the children on a trip today. The Johannesburg Zoo awaits. There is a particular gorilla, named Max, famous for once apprehending a robber who was escaping through the zoo. The robber shot Max in the jaw, but Max continued to hold him until the police came. Thembi cannot wait to lay her eyes on the bravest animal in Johannesburg.

Constance and Matlhomola wait patiently while the children get bathed and dressed. The parents smile, almost as if they are just as excited for the children to meet Max the gorilla.

"Your father and I are going to walk you to school today," Thembi's mother says. It is not common for both of them to escort the kids to school, but her mother's sentence is not a question, so Thembi does not dare say anything in response.

The children must be on the bus slightly earlier today. The field trip is scheduled to run for the entire day with a break for lunch. Thembi and Mpho board the bus. They take their seat towards the back. They look through the window with confusion as they see the two parents still standing there, watching them, waiting for the bus to roll on, almost as if they are going off to the army. Something feels odd, but the excitement to see South Africa's most famous gorilla overrides any suspicions the children may have. Constance and Matlhomola watch the bus until the handbrake sighs, the driver turns up the gospel on the radio and the vehicle of excited children disappears over the horizon. Only then do they turn around and head back for Mohapi Street.

The sun rolls itself across the sky, the hours pass, animals are watched, juice is drunk, and at the end of it all, the teachers gather the students and herd them back to the bus. Thembi and Mpho are exhausted by the time the bus gets back to Mohlakeng and parks.

They drag their feet on the walk back home, fantasising about the sleep that awaits them. However, as they approach the house, something feels out of the ordinary. There is more noise in the air around their street than usual. They walk a bit further and see a car parked at the curb. In front of it is another car, and another one after that. In fact, as they look around, they see that there are cars everywhere. Mohapi Street is by no means a quiet place, but never before have the children seen so many cars blocking the road. They walk further towards their house. As they get closer, it becomes clearer that the centre of the commotion seems to be their home. There are people everywhere, crowding every corner of the property and even spilling out onto the street. Drunken merriness fills the air, and outside the house is a giant tent, one that was most definitely not there in the morning when they left for their school trip. Thembi approaches one of the elders she recognises, one whom she knows does not mind answering questions from children,

"What is happening in this house?"

The old man looks down at Thembi with puzzled amusement,

"Oh, nothing my child. It's just that your mother and father are getting married today."

Thembi and Mpho shoot each other a look of impossibility. They cannot believe what they have just heard. They run into the house. They were with their parents just this morning and saw no hint of a wedding: There were no cars in the road and certainly no tent outside the house. It seemed like any other morning. However, as they burst through the opening to the tent, they see her standing there, next to the cake. She looks beautiful. Her white dress looks like it was sewn onto her body, perfectly fitting every curve. Thembi's mother has a smile on her face that her daughter has never seen before. Thembi also smiles at the sight of it. Her mother presses the knife further into the wedding cake, her father stands behind his bride, holding onto her shoulders with his hands and laughing from the base of his soul. The people in the tent clap as the cake is cut. It is a moment of pure, unfiltered joy.

Wedding songs are sung, old couples hold each other on the dancefloor, love is celebrated. Thembi and Mpho sneak through the maze of adult legs and find themselves at the table with the wedding cake. They sneak a piece each into their pockets and then tiptoe out of the tent, trying not to be noticed.

They take a seat against the back of the outside of the tent. They hold the wedding cake in their hands with widening eyes and salivating mouths. As they are about to take their first bites, they hear someone behind them, clearing her throat. They turn around and see the hem of a flowing white dress. They look up to see their mother, the bride. She reaches down and snatches the cake from each of the children.

"I have told you before, children are not allowed to eat wedding cake. Children who eat wedding cake will never get married."

With that, she turns and walks away, without any explanation as to why she never informed nor invited her children to her wedding. They do not ask either. They just celebrate all being under the same family banner, for the first time. The Kgatlana's are an official family unit.

CHAPTER 4

Boys and Girls

Life in Mohapi Street is intensely joyous for the youth. There are kids everywhere. Every house, every street, every playground is dotted with children, all smiling, laughing, running and playing. Thembi is one of these children. She and Mpho run circles in the dust all day until they fall down from exhaustion at night.

One day at crèche, during break, the boys are outside playing with toy cars. Inside, the teacher is taking towels and teddy bears, and wrapping them around the girls, showing them how to move around with a little one. The teacher finishes wrapping a towel around a crying girl in the corner. She stands up and turns around to look for Thembi. The teacher's eyes are met with an empty chair where Thembi used to sit. She looks outside. Thembi is playing cars with the boys. *I just thought, 'Oh damn, that looks interesting'. I wanted to do whatever it was that caused a spark in my soul. That day – it was those toy cars.*

The teacher walks out firmly, puts her arms under Thembi's armpits, brings her back to the class and sits her on a chair. She places the teddy on Thembi's back, wraps the towel around it, and ties the corners of the towel in a knot in front of Thembi's little belly, making sure she understands how it's done. Once she is through with Thembi, she stands up and walks over to tend to another child. As she bends down to tie another towel, the teacher checks back over her shoulder. Thembi is outside again. She has not removed the doll; it is still tied to her back, but she is also not about to miss playing cars with the boys.

When Thembi's mother comes to fetch her from school that day, the teacher pulls her aside.

"I am worried about Thembi. Today she only wanted to play with the boys. She was not interested in learning how to carry a baby on her back, I don't know what to do with her."

"I'll talk to her," replies Thembi's mother.

The next day, Thembi is hanging from the monkey bars, losing grip and falling often as the boys swing on by. Thembi loves falling. Her favourite part is getting up again, running to the back of the line and giving it another go. She does not give up until she makes it to the other end.

If I play on this swing, there's something within me that lights up. If I touch that car, there's that spark again. When I get to the other side of that swing, I feel like I'm on top of the world, you know? I feel like I can do anything.

MATLHOMOLA KGATLANA WALKS into his daughter's room one sunny morning. He sits on her bed and gently shakes her awake.

"Wake up, Thembi, you have school. It's your first day. Now that you're done with crèche, you need to be grown up. You need to brush your shoes and clean your socks and fix your shirt before school. I'm going to do it with you, and we're going to do it right."

Thembi yawns, stretches and smiles before doing what her father says. She follows his instructions every day and quickly learns how to tidy her room. From that day onwards, her father gets stricter and her routine becomes more filled with chores.

At seven, Thembi is still breastfeeding. *I've always been a momma's girl, but also, I think it was because I was always so tiny and hungry, so that is what she gave me – milk – when she felt sorry for me.*

One day, Thembi's father, annoyed with her breast milk obsession, tells his wife in un-minced words: "This is enough now. It stops today."

"But what must I do? She will be devastated!"

"Put plasters over your nipples and tell her that Mommy is injured."

And soon, he gets his wish and the breastfeeding stops.

It is at this same delicate age that Thembi finds herself in the back of a police van for the first time. Thembi naturally finds herself drawn to the boys and their way of playing – the wrestling, punching, kicking and running. During one of these rough sessions, a boy, tired of being outmuscled by Thembi, runs up and shoves her from behind. Thembi is on the floor before she even knows she is in a fight. As she presses up off the ground and slaps the dust off her body, she turns to see the perpetrator hightailing it in the opposite direction. Thembi crouches and grabs a rock. She closes her left eye and pulls her shoulder back before launching the rock towards the escaping boy. Unfortunately for him, he turns to look at Thembi at the exact moment the rock is due to meet the back of his head. The boy stops running, his hand goes to his eye, and he feels the blood trickling down his face and onto his arm. He pulls his hand away and notices the pool of blood on the floor. He bursts out crying. Thembi tries to apologise, but the boy is already in full sprint again and only a few steps from the teacher's office. Thembi cannot hear what he is saying to the teacher, but she can see the crying, bleeding boy in the office, and he has not stopped pointing at her since he started snitching. Three teachers come marching towards her where she is sitting on the floor, all but accepting her fate.

"Thembi! Are you crazy? You could have killed Kabelo!"

Thembi's misfortune grows as a police van happens to be patrolling the area, driving very slowly along the road next to the playground. One of the teachers standing in the disciplinary circle around Thembi walks towards the police car, and extends one hand outwards, while keeping the other hand closed behind his back. The van stops, and the teacher strolls to the window with easy casualness. He leans into the van, says a few words and points back in Thembi's general direction. Thembi begins to cry as she hears the metallic click of doors opening and the crunch of police boots hitting the ground. The officers motion towards her. She hugs her knees tighter, wishing to be invisible.

The officers say not a word as they wrap their granite hands around her tiny arms. They lift her off the ground and carry her back towards the police van. It is 1pm. There is an explosion of activity and noise as the bell sounds for lunch. One sound, however, is distinguishable above the rest, and that is Thembi kicking, crying and screaming as two men in navy blue uniform toss her into the back of the van before slamming it shut and locking the door. Thembi's tiny fingers can be seen poking through the holes in the cage at the back, and her sobbing echoes through. The policemen drive the car around the block twice before returning to the school. They open the back of the van and ask Thembi if she has learnt her lesson before letting her go.

IN GRADE 3, THEMBI IS A miniature child, an ant among beetles, a smiling and fearless ant, nonetheless. When athletics day rolls around, she is not shy to sign up for any and every event.

The gun for the 200 metre sprint goes bang, and Thembi takes off. Children stumble and trip around her, but Thembi runs on. The other girls shout something, but Thembi can't hear it. She only hears the wind as every stride takes her further from the pack. The boys on the side-line suddenly stop talking and turn to see the tiny girl with toothpick legs cross the line several seconds before her gasping competitors. One of the boys drops his chips, "Is that a girl?" Thembi finds herself having to answer that question often. *I didn't have the breasts to prove otherwise, so the only way people knew I was a girl was by me saying so.*

Thembi naturally slides into circles of boy friendships. She can match them on every level: speed, strength and naughtiness – anything. Thembi isn't interested in gossip or the other things a young girl is allowed to do to pass the time. *I wanted to glide. To be in the rain. To do all the things the boys wanted to do.* Thembi's parents reprimand her, they urge her to adopt more feminine habits, but as soon as she's back at school, she is back to playing.

When athletics season comes around again, one of the sports

teachers, Mrs Mongadi, does something unusual. She picks the boys and the girls to run together during the track meets, instead of separating them as is usually the case. As Thembi rounds the third corner of the 400 metre sprint and leaves yet another boy in her dust, she notices something. *There is actually no difference in ability between me and these boys. There's nothing they can do that I can't do just as well – or even better.*

One day, Thembi comes home with a medal. The chunky gold coin on a striped ribbon hangs heavily around her thin neck. Thembi's mother slowly turns around from the stove, and her father gently drops his newspaper. They look at their daughter and then back at each other and then back at their daughter again.

"Where did you get that from?"

"What?"

"That thing around your neck."

"It's a medal."

"For what?"

"For running."

"Go give it back."

"To who?"

"To whoever you stole it from."

"But I didn't steal it from anyone."

"Well, there's no way you won it by running."

"Why not?"

"Because I am your mother and I've never seen you run before."

Thembi bursts out chuckling and holds her medal tight. "I promise, Mom, it's all me. Look – here is the certificate!"

Thembi's mother leaves the stove and grabs the certificate, studying it closely. "Hundred metre champion! Look at you!"

Thembi's dad doesn't speak much. He sits in the corner, and absorbs what his daughter is saying while nodding his head slowly. He understands that his daughter is probably fast even though he too has never seen her run. She comes from a long line of athletes. He was a fine footballer in his day, and his wife was lightning quick around an athletics track too.

Thembi attributes her incredible speed to one tool – the sjambok.

The plastic and leather beast that reaches up into the sky before whipping down onto the ground is a common weapon used by Thembi and her friends to terrorise one another. One needs quick feet and light legs if you want to avoid the sting of the sjambok. The gate to Thembi's house is always open, but Thembi still often has to scale the side wall into the property when she's sprinting away from a whip-wielding boy.

As Mohlakeng rolls over from sizzling hot to frigidly cold and back again, a new sport is introduced. And wherever there is a new sport, there is Thembi. Often the smallest child, in the most oversized shirt, standing in the front of the line with no fear in her eyes. At one point, she even tries out baseball, and shortly afterwards she is the only girl in the school gumboot dancing club. Her collision course with football is inevitable.

CHAPTER 5

Cruel Bathrooms

By the time Thembi is in Grade 5, there are just five minutes a day she is not around boys, and that is when she needs the bathroom. In the afternoon, the boys have put down the soccer ball, and the dust has settled on the pitch. By this stage Thembi is a regular feature in the boys team. She looks around; no one is paying attention to her, so she makes her move.

Thembi has always been fast, so dashing in between all the little bodies lazing around school is no problem. Thembi approaches the hall where she knows she has to make a decision that is going to end in her being ridiculed. She steps sharply to the left and slides into the small crack in between the wall and the door that has a drawing of a skirt on it.

Once inside the cold, tiled, smelly bathroom, Thembi sticks to the wall and sucks in deep breaths as she tries to steady herself from her playground sprint. A tap slowly squeaks closed in the corner of the room. A young girl looks at Thembi over her shoulder and begins to giggle. One giggle turns into a group cackle as two more girls step out from a cubicle.

"Why are you in the girls bathroom?"

"If you want to play like a boy, you can go pee like a boy too."

"No boobs. No bum. No legs. What you gonna do in this girls bathroom?"

Thembi lifts her chin, pulls her shoulders back and peels herself off the wall. She starts walking. The giggles grow louder, but Thembi is not going to utter any words to them. Today, Thembi is going to talk with her feet. She keeps walking. She goes about her business and leaves in her own time, almost as if the other girls were never there.

Thembi walks out of the bathroom and into a much bigger and more significant moment than she realises at the time. There are five minutes left of break and the boys have started playing again, without her. Thembi kicks her little legs into gear, wheelspins and heads off for the field. As she enters this field, the ball is coming down the left wing, Thembi is shouting for it. She is barely visible under the wall of boys running back to defend the attack. The ball gets crossed wildly towards Thembi, who is charging down on the goal (two dustbins placed a metre apart). Thembi watches the ball sailing in mid-air and sees clearly that it is going to pass behind her. She swivels on her heels, turns, jumps up into the air, propelling her little body horizontal to the ground before hammering it home with a sweet bicycle kick – the holy grail of goalscoring techniques.

The playground erupts. Children swarm around Thembi, touch her head, pull her shirt, pat her back and tell her how crazy that was. As the rings of celebration circle around Thembi, there is one man at the back with folded arms, silently watching. His name is Mr Poee, and he is the coach of the school boys football team. He knew of Thembi as a runner. It is hard not to know of Thembi as a runner – she is damn fast. But today is the first time he has seen Thembi with a ball at her feet. He unfolds his arms and marches over to Thembi, places a giant hand on her shoulder, and turns her around to face him.

"You're Thembi?"

"Yes."

"How would you like to come play for the boys team?"

"The boys team?"

"Yes."

Thembi squints in confusion and looks around the playground, mostly littered with boys.

"But... I am playing for the boys team."

"No, I mean a real team."

"A real team?"

"Yes, a real team. Practices, drills, tactics, outsmarting the enemy, you know?"

"I guess…"

"Good, I'll tell Coach Maniki to expect you for practice this evening. Don't be late."

That day Thembi walks to her friend Junju's house. He lives near where the team practises. As they walk, they chatter and kick stones, not really paying attention to their surroundings. But as soon as they arrive at the pitch, Thembi stops. She looks up at the gravel field – and her jaw drops. *Once I set my eyes on that pitch, that's when I fell in love for the first time. There was no looking back from that point.*

Coach Maniki works his players. The team is called Napoli FC. It's the first real team she has ever played for. Coach Maniki cares little of the fact that she is a girl. The boys had been to training many times, so they are familiar with the process. As they begin to warm up, Thembi looks confused. Coach Maniki puts his pen behind his ear and makes his way over to the little girl. He puts his hand on her head and turns her around to face him.

"Now listen here, little girl, I didn't come fetch you from school today. You came and walked here by yourself. If you are here, you will be treated the same as the boys. If you think you can do it, then you have to show it."

Coach Maniki keeps his word. If the guys run five laps, Thembi runs five laps. If the guys do sprints, Thembi sprints too. She does not even care what any of the boys or Coach Maniki thinks. *I mainly wanted to prove to myself that anything they could do, I could do.*

Sometimes she lags behind, sometimes she falls from the pack, but she never gives up – Thembi never stops moving.

THEMBI IS IN WITH THE TEAM, but another thing she is in is big trouble. Her parents are not willing to tolerate the foolishness of their daughter playing soccer.

"It will only distract her. She should focus on other things. Girls don't play soccer, and that is the end of that."

Thembi continues to play, but her parents' concern only grows. They just do not like the sight of it, Thembi hanging around the boys all day, playing on the outskirts of the community where no one knows what they get up to. Thembi, Mpho, Bosi and Simphiwe are a pack. They are seldom seen apart. They love playing, especially wrestling and fighting. Thembi has no interest in standing by while the boys have all the fun. She takes her punches and sends them back fearlessly. The gang always walk the same route home from school together.

One late winter afternoon, as Thembi's mother stands in the kitchen, wiping down a plate, she looks up through the window and sees her daughter walking with the three boys. They stop in front of the house. Thembi is clearly talking with passion, using her hands to make her point. A commotion breaks out among the kids and Thembi goes straight for Bosi, the smallest one in the group. She throws him a vicious right hook, hoists him up onto her shoulders, spins him around – and slams him into the ground. Thembi's mother shouts out in shock, drops the dishcloth and runs outside.

"Thembi! What are you doing? Are you crazy? How can you fight with boys?"

"But he hit me first! I was just hitting him back."

Thembi's mother takes her inside, but this does little to put the young girl off her troublesome path.

THERE IS ONLY ONE DAY when Thembi does not play soccer. When Thembi wakes up in the morning, she can't find the trousers that she usually wears to school. She looks everywhere but still finds nothing. When asked if she has seen them, her mother stays silent, facing away from her. Slowly, she turns around, stretching a gym skirt from one hand to the other.

"Today, you will wear this to school."

There is no discussion. Thembi wears the skirt, but she is unhappy about it. Thembi does not speak to a single friend, and she does not kick a soccer ball. She sits at the back of the class, folds her arms on the table and then steadies her head on top of those arms and sleeps for the whole day. Or at least she tries to. When she goes to the bathroom, the other girls have something to say.

"Oh, finally you are wearing a skirt. It seems you might be a girl after all. Look at those legs though, a strong wind could snap them."

Thembi, not easily disheartened, survives the day and carries on training the next. She also carries on being reprimanded. Whenever she comes back from school with dirt on her clothes and grazes on her knee, she gets a beating.

The next day, Thembi's mother pulls her outside and takes her through the gruelling process of brewing umqombothi.

"Why do I have to know this?"

"In case you have to take over the family business one day."

"But... I am going to be a professional footballer."

Thembi's mother erupts into hearty laughter. "I better teach you just in case."

In the days that follow, Thembi shows little interest in brewing umqombothi and continues to play football, so her parents take the bold step to ground her. It works up to a point but eventually Thembi slithers out of the house like jelly refusing to be kept in a bottle.

"What are we gonna do?" asks Thembi's mom.

Her father just shrugs: "I don't know!"

Thembi's mother locks the front door.

"This will show her!"

Later that afternoon, while Thembi's mother is knitting and singing a tune, Thembi holds her breath as she slowly pushes her bedroom window open. She first throws out her bag and then slides out her little body. She looks around, grabs her bag, skips off towards the road – and exhales.

There is only one place she is thinking of heading – to the gravel to play soccer with the boys. The kids kick around until the lazy sun starts painting the field orange. With a couple of goals under her belt, Thembi heads home at her happiest. *I thought I was smart, that I had figured the whole thing out. When I got home though, I was met with a closed and locked window... Damn.*

Thembi sneaks around to the front door. She breathes deeply and then slowly opens it. Hair by hair she inches her head into the room while keeping her body safely behind the door. She peeps around the door. Both her parents are standing there, hands on hips and scowls on faces.

"Oh, this child just loves to get beaten!"

It will be a story that they will tell for many years to come. After that, her parents try a different tactic – to give up altogether.

CHAPTER 6
The Trouble Twins

Thembi loves drawing. When asked what she wants to be one day, she naturally says that she wants to be a professional footballer, but when people laugh and then ask her what she *really* wants to be, she suggests that she would be good at something artistic. Something creative but practical, like a designer of sorts. Thembi flexes her creativity through drawings of wolves and Mickey Mouse. Wolves are her speciality though. She draws dozens of them and sticks them on the door of the room she shares with Mpho, the wolf energy inspiring bravery.

When Thembi's mother finds the drawings on the door one day while cleaning the house, she rips them off and throws them away. She does not do it to be nasty; she simply wants a clean house. The elders in Thembi's life actually welcome her drawing; it is just about the only time she sits still while the sun is up. Thembi's art is a great distraction from her mischievousness.

Thembi manages to mask her naughtiness most of the time, charming adults with good manners and obedience into trusting her. But when she is left with an audience of just other children, her naughtiness knows no bounds. On Tuesdays, Thembi's class has maths after break. Before class, Thembi tells the other students that she has been deputised by the maths teacher to make an announcement.

"Teacher is busy, she is caught up in meetings."

Thembi says the official order is to chill out.

Of course, no such order actually came through. Thembi just wants to bunk class, and she does not want to go down alone. When the maths teacher is through with writing his sums on the board, he turns around to extract an answer from the class. He drops his chalk onto the floor as he surveys the clump of empty desk chairs in front of him.

"Where in the world are my students?"

Meanwhile, as the English teacher is about to enter her classroom she spots something from the corner of her eye that makes her stop. She pulls the key back from the door and walks towards a group of about 30 students relaxing in the sun, playing with grass and laughing at one another.

"What is going on here?"

Twenty-five of the students get up and bolt in different directions, leaving little clouds of dust in their wake. Thembi and four other students stand in a row. It is too late for them to escape now. They cross their hands sheepishly in front of their bodies and they stare down at the ground.

"Where are you supposed to be?"

"Maths, Ma'am," one of the students mumbles, barely audible.

"And who exactly is the mastermind behind this plan?"

The children fall even quieter and stare down harder at the ground.

"Thembi, was this you? Are you behind all of this?"

Thembi furiously shakes her head. The others furiously nod theirs. The teacher reaches out, grabs Thembi by the arm and marches her to the maths classroom, only releasing her grip on the young girl's arm once they're in the doorway.

"I found the reason for your missing class," she tells her colleague.

"Well, well, well…" As the maths teacher approaches her, Thembi makes a small calculation in her head. She realises she is probably one visit to the principal's office away from having football taken away from her. *My next move should be a bold one. There is no getting out of trouble now, so I may as well double down.* As the teacher is about two steps from Thembi, she turns and bolts. She runs straight out of the schoolgrounds and spends the rest of the day hiding behind large objects found lying around Mohlakeng.

Mpho and Thembi grow closer by the day. It is difficult to tell where the one child ends and the other begins, as they stroll through Mohlakeng shoulder to shoulder with cunningly evil smiles, plotting how they are going to entertain themselves for the day. Their naughtiness tends to multiply when they are around each other. This is a major headache for Thembi's parents, who have to answer for both children when the school comes calling.

Thembi and Mpho are *those* kids. They sit as far back in the class as possible. They chew gum, they copy each other's homework and they laugh at other students when they are doing oral presentations. Thembi is something of a harmless bully. She is never cruel or unkind, but when she laughs that deep-bellied laugh at your expense, it can be brutal.

One day during geography, the teacher says he needs to slip out for five minutes to make some copies.

"Don't get up to nonsense now," he says, looking Thembi directly in the eyes.

As soon as he leaves, Mpho springs up onto his desk like a frog hopping on a branch. The class turns and looks at him. He's holding his phone, blasting out a song. He starts to dance animatedly, biting his tongue and pulling a wickedly cheeky smile. The eyes of the class are on him. They're clapping, and some have tears of laughter streaming down their cheeks. Suddenly, like a wave rolling from the back of the class, a silence grips the raucous students one by one as they notice a towering figure in the corner of the classroom. The geography teacher stands with his arms crossed and his copies hanging loosely from his hand.

"No, please, continue Mpho."

Mpho's eyes dart around the room, fixing on the door. He weighs up his options.

"Mpho, bring that phone over to me; you can get it back next week."

Mpho does not answer. Instead, he looks down at Thembi and barks a threat, "If you tell Mom and Dad about this, I will end you."

The teacher, still in the corner, has his one hand extended for Mpho's phone. Mpho springs from the desk, and with a surprising display of athleticism, he sprints in the direction of the teacher, and then right past him and out of the class, still clutching his phone.

The turn-and-run method proves a popular way to evade punishment for Thembi, Mpho and the gang.

While Mpho's naughtiness is blatant, Thembi's is more like an undercurrent. She knows how to win over the different people in her life. Some teachers think she is an angel crafted by other well-behaved angels.

The day after Mpho's jump-and-run, it is the English teacher who says she needs to step out of the class to tend to some admin. She points the whiteboard marker at Thembi and appoints the little girl as her deputy.

"Thembi, here is some paper and here is a pen. When I am gone, you become me. If any of the children make any noise in this class, write their name on the list. If someone gets up from their desk while I'm gone, write their name on the list. If someone is breathing too loud, write their name on the list. Got it?"

Thembi flashes an angelic smile and nods innocently.

The teacher puts her hand on Thembi's head before leaving. "Good girl."

Thembi stands at the front of the class like a corporal in the army, with her shoulders back and her chin up. She paces up and down the class tapping the pencil against the top of the paper for dramatic effect. Thembi cranes her neck to see the teacher disappearing around the corner. As soon as she does, Thembi begins to orchestrate the chaos. She crunches up a sheet of paper and launches it at Mpho, zapping him on the side of the head. The students rise to their feet, paper balls fly through the air like arrows in a Viking movie, desks are overturned. The laughter is raucous. Thembi and her gang are at the centre of the mad half of the class, while the other half of the class stay seated, watching their naughty peers, shaking their heads in disapproval, and trying to refocus on their school task. Thembi looks out the window to see the teacher making her way back to the class. Thembi quickly ushers her friends back to their seats, they pick up all the paper, and Thembi quickly scribbles down a list of names on the naughty sheet.

The teacher stops in the doorway and lifts an eyebrow. She senses something in the air. The stench of misbehaviour lingers like microwaved fish. She looks at Thembi, but the little girl offers no words. She just hands over the sheet of paper. The teacher studies it carefully. The wrinkles on her forehead deepen as she reads the list from top to bottom and then bottom to top, making sure that her eyes are not betraying her. She looks at Thembi and tilts her head to the side.

"Are you sure these are the kids that were misbehaving?"

"Yes, Ma'am, absolutely. They were uncontrollable."

On Thembi's list is the name of every good, quiet and studious child in the class. The kids who have never been in detention or reprimanded in any way, because they actually behave. Nowhere on the list are the names of Thembi, Mpho or any of their accomplices.

Mpho is also one of the smokers. Thembi is with Mpho everywhere they go, but she does not light up. She enjoys her fitness more than anything and won't sacrifice it just to fit in or look cool. Nonetheless, they look like bad news when they walk together down the street. After several teachers raise alarm, the headmaster has a word with Thembi and Mpho.

"Children, I am very concerned about your behaviour at the moment. I am concerned about the friends you keep and the stories I am hearing from your teachers. Thembi, did I hear that you tricked an entire class into bunking maths? And then you got all our A-grade learners given detention? And Mpho, what was this incident I hear about your phone? And don't even get me started on the smoking."

The two troubled students do not answer. They know it won't help. Instead, they stare at their feet, nod when they need to and shake their heads when they must. The headmaster continues: "No, I cannot have this. This is getting out of control. Tomorrow, I want you to bring your parents with you to school. I want to meet them. I want to have a little word with them about your behaviour. Arrive at school half an hour earlier tomorrow, so that I can have time to have a one-on-one with your father. Do you understand?

Thembi and Mpho nod, worried and understanding at the same time.

"Dismissed."

They are not their usual bubbly selves on the walk back home from school.

"What are we going to do, Mpho?"

Mpho places a cigarette between his lips and lights it. "I mean, what can we do Thembi?"

"Well, what we cannot do is tell Mom and Dad. I know what will happen. If they hear that I have been misbehaving, they will make sure I never play football again."

Mpho shrugs his shoulders. They carry on home, report nothing to the parents, bath and then go to bed.

When the two cousins wake the next morning, they immediately sit up and look at each other. They do not need to say anything, they know that deep trouble awaits. They are particularly quiet when getting ready for school, Thembi's mother asks if everything is okay. They mutter something about being nervous for a test. Thembi's mother crosses her arms and stares at the children. An uncomfortable silence fills the space between them. She extends an eyebrow, almost as if to signal that she knows something is up, she was not born yesterday. This is the children's opportunity to speak out. They understand what her silence means as well as she does, but they cannot find it in themselves to confess. They say goodbye to her, promise to behave and head out the door.

"Boy, we're really screwed now."

"You can say that again."

"The headmaster is going to ask why we never brought our parents."

"I know."

"We need to come up with a plan."

"I know."

The two cousins walk on, but slow the pace. They are in no rush to make their appointment with the headmaster's wrath.

"Hey, look over there!" Mpho says, grabbing Thembi by the arm.

"Over where?"

"There, sitting on the corner, isn't that Mike?"

"Crazy Mike from the corner? Of course, where else would he be?"

"I have an idea."

The two children approach the old man. He is seen here often, almost as if he were cemented into the corner when they built the sidewalk. He knows everyone in the community, but not everyone knows him. This plays perfectly into Thembi and Mpho's plan. The two cousins move in on the man, and they have a hushed word, making sure that no one can overhear them. Mike listens to the children, affording them the respect of fellow adults. Once they are through talking to him, he simply and respectfully says, "I'm sorry kids, but I cannot help you."

Mpho reaches in his pocket and pulls out a crumpled-up green note. He looks at Thembi and nudges her. She does the same, fishing the R10 note out of her school bag. They hand over the two notes. Mike studies them carefully before putting them in his pocket while rising from his throne on the street corner.

The principal's office is an intimidating place. The chairs feel like they are bigger than they should be, the bookshelf is daunting, and the posters preaching discipline and sacrifice are telling. The headmaster sits at his desk, absorbed in his leather chair. He wears a look of confusion on his face.

"Are you… Are you the father of Thembi and Mpho?"

Mike takes a long, slow sip of the coffee the headmaster's assistant just made. He returns the cup to the saucer before smacking his lips and letting out a satisfied groan, as if it were the first sip of coffee he had ever had.

"Yes, yes! That is me. It is I. They are them, they are mine. Flesh of my flesh, blood of my blood, and bone of my bone."

"Oh, okay. Well, that is good. I mean, I hate to have to call you in like this, Mr Kgatlana, but unfortunately Thembi and Mpho's behaviour of late has been, well... let's just say deplorable."

Mike takes another sip of his coffee. "Hmm, yes, deplorable." He lets the word linger in the air and repeats it three times, trying to contemplate all its meanings.

"Well, Sir, I can tell you that *deplorable* was not how they were raised. They were raised very *plorably*."

The frown on the brow of the headmaster deepens. He suspects that something about this situation is shaky, but he can't quite figure out what it is.

"Well, Mr Kgatlana, our attempts at discipline have fallen flat here at the school. So I put it to you now, how do you intend to discipline these children so they do not end up becoming wasted members of our community?"

Mike finishes the rest of his coffee with an aggressively loud slurp. He stares at the headmaster for a moment before pushing himself to his feet and turning around to face the two cousins.

"Thembi, Mtho, I am very disappointed in you."

"Um, it's Mpho."

"Never interrupt me again! I gave you your name. I can change it when I like. I raised you two to be good, well-mannered, god-fearing, law-abiding, homework-doing children, and this is how you pay me back? No man, no. When we get home we are going to sit down with your mother and have a serious chat."

Thembi and Mpho bury their faces in their shirts. They aim to look as though they are hiding out of fear, but really they are trying to suppress a potential outburst of laughter. They cannot believe how into character Mike has got.

Mike inspects the mug to see if there's any coffee left. It is empty though. His next sigh is a disappointed one. He places the cup back on the headmaster's desk.

"Well, Sir, I can tell you with certainty that you won't be getting any more trouble out of these two. Tonight over dinner, we are going to have a serious discussion about family values. Now, if you would excuse me, I have surgery to perform."

Mike turns and walks out of the headmasters office, R20 richer and never to be seen by Thembi and Mpho again.

CHAPTER 7

Cops Come Visit

The family umqombothi business is booming. The house sees a constant flood of regulars as well as some people just passing through. Of course, as the drink sinks lower, the quarrels rise.

"Hey man, I have no money today. Get my beer for me, and I will have money tomorrow."

"No man, you always do this to me."

These are common words heard in the house. Sometimes these words spill over into shoves and punches. Thembi does not retreat in fear when fists start to fly and glasses start to break. She finds it all very exciting and entertaining, and she knows her father will not take long to extinguish the conflict.

One day in 2008, as Thembi is rounding the last corner before her house, she sees something that makes her shoes pause. A man is frantically climbing over her house wall, not to get in, but to get outside. Another man climbs over after him, clears the wall and runs off down a side street, a third one follows him. Thembi grips her backpack tighter as she approaches the house. As she enters the gate she sees her mother, pressed up against the side of a police car, hands cuffed behind her back. In the background she can hear her father remonstrating with the officers, but he too is in the process of being clicked into a pair of handcuffs.

The officers are not replying to anything her father says, except

Cops Come Visit

to mutter the odd word about liquor licences. An officer fetches three large drums of umqombothi from the house and pours them out onto the pavement in full view of the curious community. Thembi sits patiently to the side as she watches her parents get loaded into the back of the police van, along with a few unlucky or overweight customers who did not manage to escape when the blue lights and sirens pulled up to the gate.

Thembi's parents get off with a warning and decide to cool off for a while and close the family business.

Thembi's mother sits at home for a few days and begins to grow bored without a business to run. One day she overhears that a school from out of town is coming to visit.

"They are going to be competing in all sports: soccer, running, netball, you name it. It's going to be a good day, why don't you come, Constance?" someone asks her at church.

Thembi's mother thinks about it. She knows Thembi will be playing soccer. She also knows there is not a thing she can do to stop it. So she decides to go and watch.

Thembi's mother and uncle head off to the school. Thembi is due to play in the first of two games. She begins by playing for the girls team, and she demolishes her opponents. She zigzags through helpless flailing legs and scores five goals. A crowd gathers just to watch the little girl in the oversized shirt dominate the field.

The girls' game ends, and the boys demand that Thembi sits on the bench for theirs. The coach obliges. It is a gruelling affair. The two schools are deadlocked at 1-1. The coach sends Thembi on, just to see what happens. She gets stuck into the action immediately, amping up the game, but the clock is ticking. Right at the death, the ball goes out for a corner kick. Thembi puts her hand up to take it and jogs off to the corner spot. She places the ball down, takes a few steps backwards and catches her breath. She can feel everyone watching her: the teachers, the students, her teammates. Thembi can feel her mother in the stands, she can feel her eyes watching her and it weighs heavily on her young shoulders. She knows she has to make it count. She takes a quick skip and hops into a jog. She keeps her eyes on the ball and puts her foot through it, hoping to deliver the sweetest cross of her life.

The ball sails high; it's got a definite curve on it. Thembi's teammates and the defenders of the other school jostle in the box, waiting to time their jump perfectly, picturing that pin-accurate header that will write their names into school legend forever. The ball increases in pace and curvature. The boys jump up to meet it. It flies past every single one of Thembi's teammates' heads – no one touches it. Then it flies past the goalkeeper's outstretched fingertips, and then it curls inside the far post and ripples through the net. The physics are almost impossible, not many players in the history of football can say they have ever scored a goal directly from a corner kick – but today Thembi Kgatlana becomes one of the few.

As soon as the ball rolls down the inside of the net, Mohlakano Primary School erupts. Spectators leap out of their seats, and Thembi's teammates surround her.

"Yes Thembi!"

"You saved us!"

Between the pats and hugs, Thembi looks up into the stands. *I looked at the smile on my mom's face and I realised then that I can do a lot with a ball at my feet. I heard that girls don't play soccer. I don't know if I heard right.*

When Coach Maniki looks back at his time coaching Thembi in his otherwise all-boys team, he shines with pride.

"When Thembi was younger I always used to bring her on as a sub," he recalls. "She was also trusted with taking our penalties, to win the game for us. I played her as a striker – she always used to score. She left her opponents in her wake no matter where we played, whether it was in Kagiso, Mohlakeng, Soweto.

"There was one tournament in Mogale City where people did not believe that she is a girl. They kept asking if she is a girl. That is how she played. The way she used to run with the ball, you couldn't believe it. The way she used to bamboozle defenders. She used to work hard for the team. I trusted her all the time. Thembi was not afraid to ask for tips on how she could improve, whether it was her shooting or dribbling, and I was always happy to help her. I always had this feeling like she was going to make our township very proud one day."

CHAPTER 8

They Pay Her?

From the moment that ball hit the back of the net, Mohlakeng starts humming with chatter. People passing one another on the way to the shops ask if the other has heard of the little girl, named Thembi, who plays soccer like she is from another planet. The girl who dances with the ball and makes the boys dizzy in their attempts to keep up with her. The girl with the confidence to score the kind of goal most professionals can only dream of. Have you heard of Thembi?

Soon after the game, a local recruiter shows up to Thembi's house. He tells her of a local women's team – Parma Ladies FC. Thembi has never heard of them. She has never heard of any official all-women team in South Africa. The man says that he sees a bright future for Thembi and invites her to the next training to get a feel for the scene. She says yes, of course, and barely sleeps that night, thinking of all the things she can do with her feet.

When Thembi shows up to her first training session with Parma Ladies FC, she is out of her depth in every way. In size. In experience. In attitude. The other players are some of the most lethal women footballers in the country, and Thembi is 13 years old.

As the women start practising, Thembi notices something that she soon realises she has never see before. *It was crazy. This was the first time that I could see a women's team was possible. Not just a bunch of girls who play soccer, but an actual squad of* talented, disciplined women who could trap a ball, pass, score. Women who were built for this, you know?

Thembi holds up well at the practice, despite the fact that she is playing against the best the country has to offer. *You might not believe me if I tell you that Portia Modise was there. I got to train with Portia Modise when I was in Grade 7.*

Portia Modise is a once-in-a-lifetime kind of footballer, like Lionel Messi or Cristiano Ronaldo. Born in Soweto, she is one of a handful of footballers, men and women, to score over 100 goals for her country. She is the first African player of any sex to accomplish such a feat, and here she stands, towering over Thembi. Her hands are on her hips. She looks confused, staring down hard at the little girl.

"Who are you, little one?"

"Thembi."

"Thembi?"

"Yes."

"Thembi, you are good."

"Thank you."

"I mean, like, really good."

"Oh… Uh, thank you, Portia."

"Where did you play before this?"

"This is my first time in a girls team. I only ever played with boys before."

Portia nods her head and slowly walks away. That is the last conversation Thembi and Portia will have for some time. The next day, when Thembi arrives for practice, Portia is not there. She is not there the day after that, nor the following one.

Thembi carries on training and impressing any eyes that watch her, but one day she can't take it anymore. She simply has to know.

She marches to the office, knocks on the door, pokes her head inside and demands to know what happened to Portia.

"What do you mean what happened to Portia?"

"Where'd she go?"

"Overseas."

They Pay Her?

"To do what?"

"To play football."

"For who?"

"Fortuna Hjørring, some team in Denmark or somewhere like that."

"For what?"

"For money."

Thembi drops her bag and looks at the team manager in shock. She looks down at the floor to make sure she is not dreaming, looks over her shoulders to make sure it's not a prank, and then looks back at him.

"Are you telling me that there is a Black woman from South Africa who plays in Europe and this is how she makes a living?"

"Yes. That is possible. But it's not easy."

"But not impossible, right?"

"Right, but difficult. Remember, those girls over there in Denmark and England, they have academies. Those girls have been professional since they were young. Our girls... It's tough for them. If you want to make it from here, you've got to have that special thing. That's what Portia has. It's that force. She is fearless, you know?"

A seed is planted in Thembi's mind. All she needed was a glimpse of someone else who looks like her, who comes from the place she comes from, who makes a living doing what they love. *I didn't know, at that moment, exactly what I had to do, but I knew I was going to do whatever it took. It was strange, almost as if I were being carried by the wind.*

Thembi plays for Parma Ladies for a season. Because of Thembi's under-ripe age, the club needs to print a few papers, track down a parent and secure a signature for her to play in actual games. Due to this admin-heavy process, Thembi does not play in many games, but the experience is invaluable. She sweats through plenty of difficult practices and learns how to outmuscle, outsmart and outrun older women.

However, just as Thembi is inching closer to her place in the game squad, a common football club tragedy strikes Parma

Ladies. The funds run dry, the gate gets locked and the grass grows long. All the talent and promise in the team disperse. Some take up studies while most look for jobs. Thembi decides she is going to march on.

CHAPTER 9

A Thug in the House

Mohapi Street may be a happy one, but the houses along it know pain intimately. Thembi's family home is no different. The pain begins with the community's perception of the house. The common word is that Thembi's father is not a complete man; this is on account of him not owning the house that his family lives in. It was inherited from Thembi's maternal grandmother. Some men go so far as to call him a "wife". These harsh words are not only passed by the men in the community; some of Thembi's mother's family echo these same sentiments. It is painful for Thembi. It seems like an unfair thing to pull a man apart for. Thembi's father feels the full sting of the words, and soon the pressure becomes too much for him to bear. One night he packs his things and leaves the house that is the reason for all the tormenting. He moves in with some distant relatives. There he sits, on the couch, and he thinks about the things that are important in life. He has much time and much space to think. One days he wakes up and three months have passed. He decided to go back and tell his family and his wife that he is not going anywhere. Let the ridicule rain down – he is here to stay. *My dad knew little peace at that house. Other people accused him of lacking strength, but I know what his superpower was: keeping our family together and not running away like so many other men in the community.*

Thembi's older brother was born in 1988 in Mohlakeng. Tumelo Masinga. Thembi harbours memories of looking up to her brother. She remembers him being a charming, playful and inquisitive boy. Teachers loved him when he was younger, and he was naturally protective over his little sister. However, these are distant memories that have been replaced.

Tumelo tries drugs for the first time when he is in Grade 7. He is a smooth talker but has also always had naughtiness in his veins, and it comes as no surprise when he finds himself among a group of friends passing around a lighter and a joint.

The friends begin to explore the different kinds of drugs available on their streets, and they soon discover that if they are to keep using, they need money.

Tumelo sits quietly at the back of the English class. He is barely paying attention to what the teacher is saying. His eyes wander through the window and he thinks of being somewhere, anywhere else. The teacher excuses herself to go to the bathroom. Tumelo notices she has left her bag behind on her chair. Tumelo stands up, looks around and quickly prances to the front of the class. The other students gasp in horror as Tumelo unzips the bag and starts sifting through its contents. He removes a big leather wallet and puts it in his pocket. He takes a knife from his other pocket and turns to face his classmates. He gives a short but passionate speech, warning that should anyone tell the teacher about what he has done today, they will die for it.

After school, once Tumelo has had time to remove the cash from the wallet, he goes to an abandoned building and buries the wallet under some dirt there. One of the girls in his class sees him burying the wallet and tells the teacher. The staff at the school want to make an example of Tumelo because of the seriousness of the crime. They call the police in, they arrest Tumelo and take him away. Thembi's parents are called into a local court to explain how Tumelo is as a family member at home. Constance cries as she sees her son in handcuffs. Tumelo is sentenced to serve one month in a juvenile prison.

When Tumelo leaves the juvenile centre he returns to Mohlakeng and makes a promise to his parents, family and teachers that he will be better behaved.

"I have learnt my lesson, I promise," he says.

His friends are curious and ask him about his experience in prison. He remains coy with the details. A few months later, Tumelo walks with three of his most troublesome friends. The sight of the four boys walking down the street together, with their trousers long and their hats low, makes elders in the community shake their heads. They walk straight to the school, trying to walk like boys who were on their way to learn. At school, they break the lock on an old shed where all the sports equipment is kept. They remove everything, hiding the equipment in the bush initially and then taking them home, hidden under old clothes.

Suspicions are raised when a large number of people in the community begin to sport new shin pads and boots. Suddenly, the township team, which could previously not afford kits, has a set of shiny new exercise cones. The teachers, in partnership with the police, follow the trail of the equipment and ask the new owners how they came into possession of such nice things. It is not long before Tumelo's name is mentioned. Tumelo by this time has spent all the money he made from selling the stolen goods. The police visit Thembi's parents once again, put handcuffs on their 13-year-old son and take him away for the second time in a year.

Tumelo serves a short sentence again before being released. With each sentence he gets pushed further from rehabilitation and into pure survival mode. He has a different look on his face when he comes out of prison this time. What follows is a series of house robberies within the Mohlakeng community. The real professional criminals ply their trade in the wealthier suburbs closer to Johannesburg. But those who steal for survival and addiction steal within the community. Women grip their bags tighter when Tumelo walks past them in the street.

Living in a house with Tumelo is not easy. The simple house on Mohapi Street has four rooms – a kitchen, a dining room and two bedrooms. Initially, Thembi, being the youngest, has to sleep on the floor while Tumelo and Mpho share a bed. The family does not have much, but what they do have starts to go missing, item by item. *The dynamics of the family really began to shift when my brother became a thug within the house.*

There is no item off his radar. Clothing – both Constance's and Matlhomola's – disappears from wardrobes. Even shoelaces go missing. Mpho and Thembi own very few items of clothing, only the bare essentials really, but even these go missing. Plates and spoons vanish from drawers. And money evaporates from wallets. Even sentimental items – things bought by their late grandmother that could not be replaced, like the mugs and plates that only get used when visitors are hosted – one by one, all of these go missing. Anything that can be sold for any amount of money gets lifted from the house. Eventually, the parents tell Tumelo that he can no longer live in the house, they cannot afford for their things to be constantly stolen. They allow him to remain on the property though, and he stays in a shack in the garden behind the house. He grudgingly moves his things into the iron-sheet shelter outside. The night after he moves out, he steals all the house's window frames. Those window frames never really belonged to Thembi's parents anyway, but seeing them gone leaves a pain in their chest almost too great to bear. Once a window, now a void. An empty space where they once held all their dreams for Tumelo.

In Grade 9, Tumelo drops out of school, never to return. By this stage, Tumelo is a long way past his first pull of a joint. He now has a taste for Mandrax, tik, and a few other exotic mixtures. The purer, higher quality drugs are more difficult to find in the township, and are often too expensive anyway. This results in many other things being ground up and inhaled. One day, Tumelo finds himself in a group of friends about to pass around a joint. If there was one day that Tumelo should have stayed at home on, it is today. Just before rolling the joint, one of the boys produces a long, broken, dirty looking object. It is the nail of a spotted hyena, very difficult to come by. One of the boys grinds the nail up into a fine powder before sprinkling it into the joint, rolling it, lighting it and passing it to Tumelo.

Thembi, Mpho and her parents are all having dinner when Tumelo comes home that evening. It is immediately clear that something is wrong with him.

CHAPTER 10

Toughening Up

When Thembi is in Grade 8, a cinematic moment plays out in her life. An announcement reaches her ears that an envelope is waiting for her at the principal's office. She hurries down the pathway and nervously taps at the big man's door, poking her head inside.

"Come in, come in, young Thembi!"

She slides her polished shoes inside and stands nervously with her hands behind her back. In the corner is the school clerk, Raki. Thembi is used to his silent presence. Usually burying himself in whatever task is in front of him, Raki takes his job seriously but does not often feel the need to add to a conversation.

"A letter arrived for you today."

"Yes sir."

"Do you want to read it? I don't want you getting too excited though, okay?"

"Yes sir."

The principal hands over the letter and sits back in his chair with a big huff. The emblem on the front of the letter is as recognisable as a mirror. Two circles next to each other with inexplicable stripes running through them. The left circle is black and has an old-school football, while the right is a golden emblem of the map of South Africa. The badge evokes mixed emotions among the country, but on that day Thembi is delighted to see it. "The South

Toughening Up

African Football Association (SAFA) would like to officially invite Miss Thembi Kgatlana to come and train with the South African Girls' National under 17 squad."

Thembi lowers the letter and wants to scream, but no noise comes out of her mouth. She grips the letter so tightly that it crumples.

"Now now, steady down little girl, read on."

While keeping her eyes on the principal. Thembi slowly lifts the letter to her face again.

"Thembi will be required to train with the squad and stay in camp for the duration of two weeks. Please make arrangements for Thembi to be excused from school for this period. We thank you for assisting the national project."

"Forget. About. It."

"But, Sir?"

"I don't want to hear it, Thembi. When are you going to forget this football nonsense? A bright, young student like you should be in school. Two weeks out of class will set you back further than you can imagine."

Thembi feels that familiar disappointment, but as she holds the call-up letter to a junior national team in her left hand and stands before an unwavering principal, it stings worse than ever.

Raki, silent up to this point, slowly puts his pen down in the corner and turns to face the principal. He has a similar look of disappointment on his face to the one that Thembi is wearing.

"But, principal! How can you do this?"

"Excuse me? Raki?"

"How can you take this away from young Thembi? This isn't just soccer, it isn't just 'nonsense', this is something beautiful, a game we all love. A game we want to see Thembi go far in one day. This is her shot, at least let her take her shot, Principal! I've seen this girl play, she is really good."

The principal hums, winces and rubs his chin. He does not like it, but he knows he has to trust Raki. He has known him a long time and knows that he does not remonstrate loudly unless it is coming from a place of deep conviction. The principal very hesitantly agrees to allow Thembi to join the national under 17 team. Many years later when Thembi returns to her old school, Raki will never forget to remind Thembi, jokingly, of the time he fought for her, and how in some small way, she owes her career to him.

"Never forget how I fought for you, Thembi."

Putting on the national jersey at a junior level elevates Thembi to the eyes and ears of the best scouts in the country. She wears the jersey with pride, even though it is chronically oversized as the girls usually just wear the boys' old shirts. Thembi dances around her opponents and dazzles the coaches watching the game. A few days after the final whistle, she gets yet another important letter delivered.

Because of a lack of a professional women's league in South Africa, the High Performance Centre (HPC) was set up at the University of Pretoria. It is meant to act as a feeding funnel to Banyana Banyana. They take on promising talents across many sporting codes, develop them academically, athletically and mentally and send them out into the world to fly the flag high. The HPC announces that they would be delighted to take on Thembi Kgatlana as a student footballer.

Shortly after joining the HPC, Thembi finds herself on a plane for the first time in her life. The team is going to a competition in Denmark that involves boys and girls from around the world. *It was crazy for me, a girl from Mohlakeng, sitting in this fancy new aeroplane. I knew there was such a thing as aeroplanes out there, but I never thought, with the family that I grew up in, that I would ever get to sit in one. I remember the other girls were taking pictures, so many pictures. I've never really been like that though.*

Going on excursions means everything to Thembi. She feels every second on the road and spends her time with her eyes stuck to the windows, watching the world pass by. Thembi has a thirst for learning, she loves the away games in Pretoria, rural Eastern Cape, KwaZulu-Natal, or anywhere that shows her a different side of human life. *Isn't that what life is all about? Seeing how other people live, how they go about it, how they overcome difficulties in life. That's where I get my perspective from, from being exposed to other points of view. That is what I've used to build my character.*

Going to the HPC also changes Thembi's relationship with her parents. They still hold deep insecurities about their girl child going off to play football. Her dad is especially hesitant. He has not seen her play yet. He has not seen a woman play football ever. Worry is written all over his face,

"Thembi, go play soccer if you feel you have to. But just know one thing, how far you go in life or how short you come will be determined by you and only you."

"I'm going to make it, Dad. If you come watch me play, you'll see."

"I don't know…"

"Just come, Dad! Mamelodi Sundowns ladies are coming for a preseason game against us this weekend. They are the top team in the country."

"The top team? So you want me to see you getting *walloped* in your first game in front of me?"

Thembi giggles at her father's forecast.

"Just come, you'll see."

When game day arrives, Mr Kgatlana is one of the last spectators to walk into the stadium. He finds an empty seat by the touchline and sits down, with low expectations, to watch his daughter play football.

Midway through the first half, Thembi receives the ball at the edge of the box, controls it with a deft touch and then fires it off her right foot into the bottom left corner of the goal. Thembi's teammates come up to hug and high-five her. It is a controlled celebration. The celebration from Thembi's father, however, is anything but controlled. He is jumping up and down, moving between the seat and the floor. He pulls his hat off his head and waves it around, he whistles and pumps his fists, running up and down the row. He screams until every supporter in the stadium knows that Thembi is his daughter. *He went crazy, he acted like I had just scored the World Cup winning goal.*

On the drive back home, Thembi's dad speaks more than she

has ever heard him speak before. He can't stop speaking about the goal. *It's a different relationship between you and each parent. It was difficult to open up to my dad usually, but that day he was like a child.*

As they dodge and whizz through the traffic on the way home, Thembi's father begins to tell her a story.

"When I was watching you today, I was sitting next to someone who is on the coaching team for Mamelodi Sundowns, an old man. He was telling someone else that you are good. Really good, one of the best he has ever seen in his many years. He said if you didn't live so far, they would scout you, but there is no money to bring you over at the moment, but he said you were the most promising player on that field today."

Thembi absorbs every word, and her smile gets wider and brighter. She turns her face to see out the window and lifts her chin with pride from all the compliments she is hearing. Her father watches her for a moment. He sees his daughter visibly growing in confidence by the second. He reaches out to pull her back.

"Don't get carried away now, little one. You are good, yes, but you are still not good enough. Not even close. You think you are much better than you actually are."

Thembi's jaw trembles and her eyelids grow heavy. The words feel unnecessarily harsh in what is supposed to be a moment of celebration.

"If you can do this consistently for two or three years, then you will have my support, then, just maybe, you might be good enough to make it."

Thembi stays quiet for the rest of the drive home, with tears welling in her eyes. For now she only feels the cruelty of her father's words.

CHAPTER 11

Can't Come Home

From that point onwards, Thembi begins to experience criticism from her father like never before. He is particularly harsh on her in games where she plays well. A resentment builds inside of Thembi whenever the subject of football comes up between her father and her. It is never a positive conversation, and compliments are rarely, if ever, given. He sees the pain on her face, but he simply tells her that he is trying to make her stronger.

As time goes on, Thembi's father's cargo-load of criticism only intensifies. If she scores three goals in a game, her father asks what happened to the fourth one.

I had to constantly level up my attitude. Every time I reached a target he set for me, he would move it further away. It was almost as if I was competing with him, but it was more difficult than that, because I felt like I was the only one who was putting in the hard work in this competition.

THE HPC OPERATES SIMILARLY to a boarding school, but to Thembi it feels like she has been drafted into the army. The first bell slaps the ear drums at 5.30am, girls up. By second bell your boots better be on and laces tied, because training starts at 6am. At 7.30am, you eat. Finish up fast because the wheels on the bus start spinning at 8am and school starts shortly after that. Sit down and focus your hardest to decode the private school English, take notes and don't sleep. Books need to be packed and legs need to be moving by 3.30pm, the bus driver does not enjoy waiting. Strap the boots back on, loosen up, afternoon training starts at 4pm. Prove that you are one of the best in your age group in the entire country for the next two-and-a-half hours, and then get showered afterwards. At 6pm you eat. At 7pm, the books need to be out again, dusted off and ready to be absorbed. At 9pm you can relax and watch *Muvhango* with the other learners. At 9.30pm you must stop relaxing and start sleeping – you have an early start again tomorrow. Mondays particularly suck, it's weights day in the gym and Thembi automatically falls asleep in the first class. The principal complains that Thembi is too tired. She is too tired to argue back.

Everything is different for Thembi. The beds, the bathrooms, the food, the other students, it is all from a new world. The teachers and coaches monitor Thembi's progress carefully. She is not coping, and it is evident for all to see. The greatest struggle for her is the kind of English being spoken in the classes and halls. *In the kasi you just spoke English mixed with whatever. This was something completely new.*

Due to a change in government laws at the time, Thembi began learning Grade 1 at the age of 6, a year younger than the other learners in her grade in private school. When the powers that be at the HPC find this out, they call Thembi in for a meeting.

"Thembi, we've got something difficult to tell you… We are going to have to hold you back a year. You need to be with peers your age. I know you are not going to like this news, but we hope one day, when you go far in life, you will see that this decision was the right one."

"But, I have already passed Grade 10, in Mohlakeng?"

"Yes, we know. And you will pass it again. We have every faith in you, Thembi."

The dam walls on Thembi's tear ducts burst open. She turns and makes for the door. She runs far, far away from the principal's office. Thembi stops by a tree, sits down in a slump, cries some more and thinks about what she has to do. After a moment, she stands, shakes it off and marches back in the direction she came, each step charged with determination. She stops next to the school phone and looks around before picking up the receiver and darting in the numbers. Two sharp rings sound out.

"Hello?"

"Hello? Mom! I can't do this anymore. I want to leave the HPC."

"Hello?"

"Mom, can you hear me? I want to leave this place. I can't do it, I'm not cut out for it. I'll just come back to Mohlakeng and be a normal school girl."

"You what?"

"They are going to make me do an extra year of school, they want me to spend the rest of my life here!"

"You know, my child…" The phone is snatched out of Thembi's mother's hand.

"Thembi, this is your father. I am going to drop this call right now. Suck up those feelings that you are having, turn around and go back inside, and do whatever it is you have to do. Look around you. Look at the other girls. Do you see any of them complaining? No. Stop calling your mother now. You can call us on the weekends only. Do you hear me? The rest of the time, you have to get to work, and remember that whether you make it or whether you fail – it is all on you." The phone slams down the other end and flatlines an ominous tone in Thembi's ear. *That moment really prepared me for life. That taught me a lot about picking up when things get tough.*

Soon after, Thembi does settle in, and she immediately draws attention to herself. Most of the children are very quiet at first, just trying to find where they fit in. One such shy girl is Amogelang, who could do nothing but notice Thembi.

"There was just something else with Thembi," Amogelang says. "She was so 'hood', you know? There was no assessing the situation, seeing how she could fit in – she was just running up and down making everyone laugh. We all thought, 'What is the matter with this child?' She just had this hustler mentality from the get-go."

CHAPTER 12
Crazier than Usual

Tumelo enters the house, not stable in his legs, sweating, grabbing at his shirt. It seems as if he is in pain but he cannot voice it; he has lost the ability to string together words in a sentence. Thembi's parents try to give him water and bread and to ask him what he has done and where he has been. He cannot feel their touch on his shoulders or hear their words. There is a distance in his eyes, as if his mind is no longer on this earth with his body. In between the noises he makes, he manages to get enough voice out to tell his family that he is in extreme pain. They lay him down on the floor and call an ambulance.

Tumelo is stabilised in the public hospital, and after an examination, they send him to the psychiatric ward. He spends the next seven months receiving treatment. While he is in hospital, the family has time to discuss what should be done about the situation. It is a source of great conflict in the family. Thembi's father, not keen to see the boy tear apart the family that he works so hard to keep together, is particularly harsh on Tumelo. By contrast, Tumelo's uncle sympathises with him. He often challenges Thembi's father, telling him that harsh discipline will not help the boy fare any better. Thembi's mother is the one truly caught in the middle; she must sit by while her younger brother fights with her husband about her severely addicted firstborn child. Thembi feels her heart cracking for her mother but decides to stay as uninvolved in the drama as possible. Although in a house such as theirs, this is near impossible.

Once Tumelo's seven months of rehabilitation are through, he is informed that he will be released soon. Thembi knows that the treatment has helped, he has definitely come down off the high that put him there in the first place. However, Thembi notices something curious – her brother continues to pretend to be insane. More insane than usual. Thembi knows her brother well enough to know that it is an act, but the doctors are none the wiser. Tumelo gets transferred to a different psychiatric institution, and Thembi figures out his play. In Tumelo's wake he has left a lot of destruction. He robbed many people in the community, and secrets do not stay hidden in Mohlakeng for long. All of Tumelo's friends who were involved in the break-ins with him were rounded up and arrested. Tumelo knows that, should he ever leave this place, he will go straight to prison. He knows that insanity is his only shot at a normal life. He is a smooth talker and a good actor by nature, and the role of loopy comes easily to him.

He manages to drool on his shoulder and speak in slurs. He gets fed three fair-enough meals during the day and at night he plays cards. He keeps this up for a long time, until eventually, after a year, the authorities catch up with him. Tumelo is taken away from the psychiatric institution and to a court of law. Thembi's mother weeps from the gallery as the judge calls out, "Mr Masinga, please rise," before sentencing Tumelo to 10 years in prison.

Tumelo serves four of his years before being released early on parole due to good behaviour. What those four years entailed, only Tumelo knows. As he walks out of the gates of the prison he looks at the streets around him and has an honest conversation with himself. He knows that he carries with him two things, an unfinished schooling career and a criminal record, which leaves him with very few options. He walks on, step by step, off to survive again.

A few months and a couple of broken windows later, Tumelo finds himself with his face on the ground, and his hands being cuffed behind his back again. In 2010 he is taken back to court and sentenced to 15 years in prison.

CHAPTER 13

Injure One, Injure All

There is a woman who comes from Eersterust in Pretoria. She has a heart that stretches beyond all kindness. Her love of children is so pure and her attention to respect and discipline is razor sharp. When the HPC was established, this woman was hired by SAFA to act as a mentor to the young girls being groomed for the national team. She is affectionately known as Granny.

Granny is here to make focused and respectable athletes out of young, energetic girls, to make sure they never muddy the national flag when they represent their country one day.

Thembi is popular with the other students in class and often finds herself on the wrong end of a stern word. Whenever the children misbehave at school, Granny is the first one to find out.

Granny is well versed in disciplining the youth, and she hits them where it produces the greatest sting. All 25 girls line up and hand in their cell phones. The sentence is harsh every time – no phones from Sunday evening until the following Friday after school. *During weeks like this, when we were punished, the focus would be on another level. No distractions, it was just you. Training. Books. You. Training. Books.*

Granny is fond of giving speeches. The students often sit at her feet, with devastated looks dripping off their faces, listening to every syllable she utters.

"I tell you girls once, I will tell you a million times. If one of you makes a mistake, all of you will be punished. You need to get used to playing on a team. Injure one, injure all." *She used to love saying that: "Injure one, injure all." She would say it after every story: "Injure one, injure all."*

It is difficult to escape Granny. Most days, and nights, she stays with the girls in the HPC boarding house. If there's something going on, at any hour of the day, Granny usually knows about it, and shortly afterwards sticks out her hand, indicating that it is time to hand in your phone. When the girls remonstrate with Granny and tell her of how deeply unfair it is that they should get punished for one girl's naughtiness, Granny does not want to hear it.

"If you saw her doing it, and you did nothing about it, then you are also wrong. This is life, girls. Not stopping someone from doing something bad is the same as doing something bad. You cannot call yourself someone's teammate if you do not help her stay out of trouble." *So we kept each other pretty honest mainly because we all really liked keeping our phones.*

Granny puts a lot of effort into getting the group of girls bonded together as a team. Every other Sunday they have drama evening. The girls break into groups of five, have to come up with characters, make costumes and play out scenes for the other students. Thembi hates it at first. Sundays in Mohlakeng did not involve the dramatic arts. Thembi has never done drama as a subject and cannot believe that she is forced to be so humiliated in front of her new teammates. As time goes on though, Thembi realises she is not being humiliated, but rather, humbled.

Granny plays an essential role in the team, and she remembers it fondly.

"My role was to be a mother to these girls," she says. "But I was not always the mother they wanted. I was very strict. I had to learn to be strict. I learnt a lot through those girls. It was like going to school every day for me too. You see, it was a really tough thing to get them bonded. These girls all came from completely different backgrounds. There were girls there from the rural areas who only had only one pair of underwear, who had never slept in a bed before in their lives. And here they were, sharing a bed with girls who have had everything – girls who came from places where their rooms had bathrooms and they never had to share any of their things with someone else. It was a culture shock on both sides. Because everyone was so different, the only way I could bring them together was to treat them all the same. So I was strict, and not many of them understood at the time why I was the way I was, but they usually get it later on in life. They often call me up and tell me so."

The central pillar in Granny's teachings though, is respect.

"Girls, respect, is often misunderstood. Respect must never be tied to a person's title. You shouldn't just respect me because you call me Granny. Respect me as a human being. Never give more respect to a person just because they are powerful. Respect the man walking in the street. Respect the ladies who clean the school. Respect yourself."

On some Fridays the girls are allowed out. They may go to the mall, buy clothes or watch a movie, or to the park, so long as they went in pairs and told Granny where they were going before they left. *Those days really stand out. Any other day you'll see us there in tracksuits and football socks. But on these days we got to dress up nicely... Put on your jeans, some nice kicks – and actually feel like a human being for the first time in a while.*

Another thing the girls like doing – for fun – is laughing at the boys. Often they huddle on the side-line and watch them play. When the boys notice that they are being watched, they try to up the flair. This sometimes results in a boy tripping, stumbling or just generally making a fool of himself. This has the girls gripping their stomachs and swaying from side to side, infected with hysterical laughter.

The girls at the HPC never play other girls teams. There is no professional league for women in South Africa; the HPC is the highest level an aspiring girl can hope to spring her career from. *We were just so much quicker, stronger and faster than any other girls team out there. So, our coach never made us play against other girls. She never saw the point. She said we wouldn't be properly tested that way, we would not be prepared for the professional fields.*

Thembi becomes one of the loudest students at the school. Her laugh echoes down hallways and bounces off the walls into corridors. Thembi's coach at the time, Sheryl Botes, remembers it fondly: "From my office I would hear this laugh, and I would know straight away that it was Thembi. Even the first time I met her, she was this tiny girl, but there was this love and passion in her eyes. She was just so, so skilful, it was unbelievable. Her technical ability was sharp, and she had this explosive speed that other girls just couldn't deal with. She could dribble while sprinting, and when it comes to football intelligence… Well, I've never really seen anyone like her."

Thembi is constantly late. Especially for the early periods. She takes her sleep seriously, and sometimes getting out of bed feels like an impossible boulder to climb. When Thembi eventually does stroll into class, she is met with an interrogation.

"Thembi, you are 20 minutes late, how can this be?"

"I was in the toilet, Sir."

"Nobody goes to the toilet for 20 minutes, Miss Kgatlana!"

What does not help Thembi in her plea for innocence are her dreadlocks. Coach Sheryl associates dreadlocks with one thing and one thing only – weed smoking Rastafarianism. Thembi also suffers chronic headaches. Some days are worse than others. On one of the tougher mornings, Thembi's migraine is so intense, she struggles to focus. She enters the dining hall with a dazed and distant look in her eyes. Coach Sheryl is busy making coffee for Granny and herself when she notices Thembi standing in the middle of the canteen, red-eyed and lost.

"You see, Granny, you see? This is what I was telling you. This one smokes too much dagga – look at her eyes."

Thembi tries to explain to them the thumping pain that tortures her head, but still they remain suspicious. They send Thembi for a drug test before they send her to the doctor.

Granny is used to being suspicious of Thembi. She recognises the naughtiness in Thembi's eye. She finds caring for Thembi much like caring for a puppy. If she sees a group of students somewhere and Thembi is not with them, Granny knows she must go looking for her, because Thembi is definitely up to something.

One day, after yet another draining week of heavy academics and intense training sessions, the girls change into their weekend clothes and head off to the main office. They are exhausted. They drag their feet and groan, but there is one shining light that pulls them through – it is a Friday afternoon, and they are getting their phones back from Granny. The girls arrive at the office in a pack and follow their usual procedure. They quieten down, neaten up, knock on the door and call out, "Granny?" They hear nothing but silence in return.

Many kilometres away, in Eersterust, sits Granny, sipping a cup of tea while anticipating the serene peace of a childless weekend. Granny puts down her cup and looks at a sports bag filled with 25 cell phones. They will sit there for the entire weekend. Granny gives a wry smile as she pictures the disappointed faces of the teenaged girls, and the shock they must be experiencing as they gear up for a phone-less weekend.

CHAPTER 14

The Biggest Bag We Have

During the course of the season, the girls at the HPC are given a lot of clothes, mainly from their sponsors. Their school uniform is not really a uniform, as it's made up of a variety of different clothing items. At the end of every term, the girls are tasked with cleaning out their rooms. It is not uncommon for some girls to leave behind items of clothes they no longer desire; these are usually then gathered up and thrown away. Thembi felt a pain in her heart last time she saw all the clothes go to waste. So this year, just before the end of term, Thembi goes home and begs her parents to lend her the biggest bag they have in the house.

Back at school with the shelves empty and the lights off, Thembi goes to work, darting in and out of rooms, finding socks, caps and shirts that have been abandoned. She gathers them all into her bag, ties it and heads out of the school. When Thembi gets home, she hands the bag to her parents and asks for their help in washing the items. Once they have dried the next day, Thembi goes around her community handing out clothes to those in need.

Later that year, during provincial trials, Thembi sees another girl, lanky and skinny but unbelievably skilful. The girl looks familiar to Thembi, who watches her play the entire half. She sees something special in this girl. She can picture the two of them causing havoc on the field together. The girl she is looking at is Linda Motlhalo. One day she will go on to be known as

"Randfontein Ronaldinho", almost as if she were infected with the same Brazilian skill as the legendary long-haired maestro. Linda and Thembi would go on to travel the world together throughout their careers, and Linda remembers clearly the first time they met: "She was just… way too forward. So talkative. You could see, this girl was not shy. At these provincial games, none of us knew each other, but there was Thembi going around the circle talking to everyone like she had known them for the longest time. But then I saw her play, and I knew she was loud for a reason."

In 2014 the pressure really begins to mount for Thembi. She is now in matric, and in her final year at the HPC. The girls at the HPC have to be intensely focused; the stakes are much higher for them than they are for the boys. A promising boy could be snatched up by an average professional team and still make a decent living. No such option exists for a girl from South Africa. They need to hope that they can play well enough to be called up to the senior national squad. If that happens, you might be lucky enough for a foreign scout to see you during a positive run of play and then – just maybe – you might be able to make a living in women's football. However, even these odds are bleak, because as of 2014, Banyana Banyana have only just qualified for their first ever Olympics. They have yet to ever qualify for the World Cup. In an effort to create a better legacy for the national team, SAFA announces a big signing – the legendary Dutch coach and former player Vera Pauw.

This is a huge moment for women's football in the country. Never has such a sizable investment been levied nor such a bold step been taken. Thembi hears the news but thinks little about it. She is just focused on progressing out of the academy and into the big time, and the only way she knows how to do this is through hard work, and with a smile on her face, of course. Few people ever describe meeting Thembi for the first time without describing her smile.

One day her smile is particularly bright as she does the thing she loves most – playing soccer. Except, on this day she is not playing regular football, there are no cones and they stand on no field. Thembi and the boys are playing an informal game. They have put two wheeled dustbins on either side of a little slab of concrete in the shadow of one of the tall dormitories, and the game is mostly about the players trying to out-skill each other.

It is a spectacle to watch, but it is also very loud. The excitement of the game grows so much and the noise becomes so deafening that it stirs someone who is trying to relax on the third floor. The lady on the third floor takes out her earphones, gets up off the chair and peers out of the window to the game down below. She sees an excited flurry of players trying to skin one another with devious skill. The woman walks out of the room, down the stairs, out of the front door and marches towards where the students are playing, her short blond hair bouncing with every step. She stops just short of the field, crosses her arms and watches the players grinding away. Her face lights up as she watches the skill on display. Thembi only notices the woman after she scores her fifth "goal" of the day. She stares at her for a moment. The woman stares back. Thembi looks back to the ball and carries on running. The woman unfolds her arms, turns around and walks away without saying a word.

Thembi waits another week before she gets her phone back. There's a handful of missed calls and one message waiting.

"Hi Thembi, this is Levi, the manager of Banyana Banyana. Vera Pauw wants to speak to you. Call us back."

CHAPTER 15

Step Up or Step Out

Thembi has not sensed reality, not since she put down the phone. It has all been a dream. She has not yet dared to smile, scared she may chase this dream away. The principal notices Thembi's trembling hands. She puts her firm hand on her shoulder, and assures her that the news is real.

Thembi manages a small nod of appreciation at the principal and then slips out of his office. Her head remains still and her face shocked, but her legs start moving her towards class. Thembi's friend Amogelang sees her from behind and jogs to catch up. She shoulders up to Thembi, grabs her by the straps of her bag and studies Thembi's face.

"What is wrong with you now? It looks like you've seen a ghost."

Thembi turns to face her friend. Noticing her for the first time, she snaps out of her trance and looks around before leaning in to whisper in Amogelang's ear: "I just received the call-up, I think I am going to Banyana Banyana this evening to join the players in camp. I mean, that's what the guy said on the phone but I don't…"

Amogelang's cheeks inflate with excitement with every passing word, and halfway through Thembi's sentence, she explodes with joy. She jumps circles around Thembi, patting her on the back, kissing the top of her head, grabbing her shoulders and shaking her.

"You made it! You made it! I can't believe you made it."

"Relax. I haven't made anything. It was just a phone call. Time will tell if it's real."

With each passing step and with each congratulatory hug from Amogelang, it begins to dawn on Thembi that this *is* real, it has no reason not to be. Thembi packs in a rush, hardly paying attention to the things she is throwing into her bag. She is replaying the phone call with Levi in her head, picturing the details. She knows she needs to get to Pretoria, where one of the groups of potential Banyana Banyana players will be sharing a car. The car will drive to Soweto, where Vera Pauw will begin the turnaround of the South African national women's team.

Thembi is full of hope on the drive over. She pictures herself in the Banyana Banyana jersey, scoring goals, lifting trophies and receiving awards. The dream stops as the car brakes and the driver tells Thembi they have arrived at camp. As Thembi looks around, she notices that there are a lot of other girls in football kit. She goes to the first desk and signs her name on the register. She is welcomed and informed that there are 39 women already here; she is the 40th. By the time the first ball is kicked, there are 60 players on the field fighting to make their dreams come true. Vera is looking for a squad to take to the Africa Women's Cup of Nations (AWCON) – and she is only issuing 23 tickets.

Thembi has had a mere few hours' notice to prepare for this moment in her life, where she must prove herself to be one of the 23 best footballers in the country. She looks closer at the other players. She realises that this is no regular trial. She is in the presence of royalty. Juggling a ball in the far corner is Simphiwe "Shorty" Dludlu, a former captain of Banyana Banyana. Stretching on the other side of the field is Janine van Wyk, one of the 100+ capped players of this team.

I was so overwhelmed by it all. I mean, I was standing on the same field as Amanda Dlamini, Portia Modise, and my personal role model, Nompumelelo "Mpumi" Nyandeni.

Thembi's role model is a remarkable woman, who made her debut for the senior national team at the age of 14. By this stage,

Banyana Banyana have these colossal pillars in the form of these big names, who have stood the test of time, and are still in the prime of their careers. Thembi looks around the squad and appreciates the presence of greatness. She tells herself that she should not worry about competing with them, she is just here for the experience. She takes a knee, ties her bootlace and then looks up and has another thought. *What if this is one of those times in life? One of those chance moments. Those things that you fear might not ever happen again. I decided, "Nah, I'm not here for the experience – I'm here because I deserve to be here. I'm here to play."*

The first ball comes high to Thembi. She cushions it with the inside of her boot and brings it to the ground. She has a moment to look up and assess her options. It's a damp night in Soweto. Thembi breathes heavy mist. Steam rises from her shoulders up to the floodlights. She can feel Vera's eyes on her. She can feel all the other players' eyes on her. And even though her family are not here, she can feel their eyes on her too. She releases the ball, which finds her teammate with pinpoint accuracy. It's a simple play, but one that shows football maturity in high pressure situations. Vera writes on her clipboard, and then continues to pace up and down the field.

After two days, Thembi notices fewer and fewer girls at the breakfast table, and as she finds herself still sitting there, drinking juice, something dawns on her. She has received a lot of good advice in her life, and in particular from her HPC coach Sheryl Botes, who told Thembi shortly before camp, "You're absolutely dreaming if you think being good at one position is going to get you into the national team. Whose place are you going to take? You going to kick Portia out of the striker's spot? Or Shorty out the midfield? Or do you think you can take Janine van Wyk's place at the back? Never. If you do one thing by the time you leave the HPC, let it be to master at least three positions. That left foot of yours could use a lot of sharpening as well."

Three days pass. Many women leave the camp, often wiping their eyes and sniffing heavily, yet Thembi finds herself still sitting at the breakfast table. Vera slides onto the bench next to Thembi and leans in to have a covert word.

"Listen Thembi, you are not in the team just yet. When we go to the game, you will still be on trial. Just be ready when your moment comes, okay?"

Thembi smiles. She does not need to answer. The look on her face says that she is not merely ready, but more like she was born to do this.

It's 5 August 2014, a windy day in Dobsonville Stadium, Soweto. Banyana Banyana are up against Namibia in an international friendly. When it comes to game day, Thembi breathes easier. When she looks around and sees the powerful ring of women, she notes the fact that she is no longer just a fan, a little girl staring up at her idols. She now stands shoulder to shoulder with the giants. She is one of them.

Thembi starts the game on the bench. She taps her foot and watches anxiously as her teammates outmuscle and outsmart their opposition through the midday heat. Thembi keeps looking at Vera, then back to the clock, then back to Vera again. Sixty minutes pass. Vera does not look at Thembi. Seventy minutes pass, Banyana Banyana scores another goal. Vera is still not noticing Thembi. Seventy-five minutes pass. Thembi can barely sit still on the bench, and Vera is still not looking at her. At 80 minutes, just as Thembi is getting ready to park her excitement for another day, she looks up, and Vera is looking at her. She smiles at Thembi and motions for her to approach. Thembi springs to her feet and removes the substitutes bib. Vera wraps her arm around Thembi's little shoulders, leans in to her ear and points out to the field.

"Thembi, this is a perfect time to introduce you to senior international football. We are up 5-0. There are 10 minutes left. I'm bringing Portia off to rest. You go out there and get a feel for the ball."

Thembi does some quick stretches and hops from one foot to the other, waiting for Portia to come off. SAFA has just received a new sponsorship deal from Nike, but the kits sent to the women's team are no different to the kits sent to the men. Thembi is drowning in her shirt. Her sleeves go past her elbows, and her shorts, rolled up and tucked in, still cover her knees and half her shin pads. This is a disadvantage to most players, but Thembi has done this before, playing against her opponent as well as her own kit. It is no sweat to her. Portia Modise does her final wave to the fans and then jogs over to Thembi on the side-line, stretching out her hands to grab Thembi's, "Little one, just go out there and enjoy yourself."

Thembi smiles back. As she steps onto the field and looks down at the boots that are carrying her, she feels something in her heart. A feeling of completion, of circularity, almost as if a centrepiece of a puzzle has just slotted perfectly into place.

For 10 minutes, Thembi throws her bones into the game. She is fierce. She plays with the spirit of a woman who only has 10 minutes to live. She causes panic among the Namibian defence and draws admiration from her teammates and coach. The game finishes. Simphiwe Dludlu fondly remembers the intensity Thembi brought to her first game: "She was so young, sitting on the bench. She said that if she was given the chance to come on, the defender would be in trouble. I laughed at the time, but I stopped laughing when I saw that defender come off on a stretcher."

A resounding victory for Banyana Banyana is in the bag. Thembi takes a moment to appreciate her sweat and how it pours down the badge over her heart. As she walks off the field, Thembi thinks of the people who lifted her up to this point. She takes a moment to appreciate that she is sweating for her country. When Thembi looks at her boots, a scene from her life replays in her head. At the time Thembi was called up to Banyana Banyana, her parents were not in a financial position to buy her new things as she required them. While attending a church service just before the game, Thembi was pulled aside by Father Nkosinathi. He smiled and pulled something out from behind his back – a new pair of shiny football boots. "Thembi. I heard the news. And I wanted to spend my money to give you these," he said.

It was the moment that I truly realised what football could do. There was this look on the pastor's face. Father Nkosinathi knew something that Thembi was also familiar with – Mohlakeng. They both understood the place they come from, and how it thirsted for role models. They both knew Thembi could be that light for her community.

He handed her the boots and said, "Now make us proud."

CHAPTER 16

Books and Boots

After the camp, Thembi boards a bus back to the HPC. She checks her phone on the way back and sees she has an SMS,

"Thembi you made the cut, top 30! Next camp is in Zimbabwe, pack your boots – don't forget your schoolbooks."

Banyana Banyana travel to Limpopo to acclimatise to the kind of conditions they can expect to face in Zimbabwe. Thembi feels the heat of the Limpopo earth under her feet, but she also feels a different kind of heat. At this time, all across the country there are nervous matric students, burying their heads in textbooks and hoovering up knowledge, understanding that their actions over the next few months could go a long way to determining the rest of their lives.

At the same time, there is a group of women, only 30 of them. An elite squad of heroines on an ambitious mission to do what those before them have attempted but never quite achieved: get South Africa to the World Cup.

The matric students breaking pencils, and the group of elite women tying their football laces are under immense pressure – Thembi happens to be part of both groups.

What is more difficult than the exams for Thembi is being in camp with Banyana Banyana and being the only one still in school. The other players have their downtime, and they relax in the lounge. Janine switches on the TV, Amanda opens a bag of chips. The women laugh, and they talk, and they watch *Muvhango* and *Generations*, and Thembi watches from the corner of the room. Her arms are folded shyly in front of her, and she has eyes like a puppy.

"Go back!" Simphiwe Shorty Dludlu is not messing around. Thembi knows Shorty from their time together at the HPC, where Shorty is a part-time coach. It is for this reason that Shorty has been paired with Thembi to be Banyana Banyana roommates. She only knows the other players from seeing them on TV. Shorty is all too aware of Thembi's academic situation, and she does not hesitate to put Thembi in her place. She stretches her arm straight and points directly out of the room, her face is stone cold.

"Thembi, go study."

"Please can I stay?"

"No."

"Just for a little bit?"

Shorty picks up a cushion off of the couch and winds her arm back, taking aim at Thembi.

"I said no!"

Thembi giggles, turns and runs out of the room. Shorty shakes her head, stands up and walks out, leaving the other players to the soapies. Shorty takes Thembi by the shoulders, marches her to their room, and sits her down behind the desk. Shorty extends her hand to Thembi with the palm facing up. Thembi pretends not to see Shorty. She flips through her textbook and nods her head at random pages. Shorty reaches her outstretched hand even closer Thembi. Thembi looks up at Shorty, trying to engage her with puppy eyes again.

"What?"

"Your phone."

"No, please Shorty, that's crazy."

"Your phone! I never asked. Here, give it."

Thembi grudgingly slaps her phone into Shorty's palm.

"Fine. You're just like Granny, you know?"

"Ja, that's fine, I'll be your second 'Granny'. Now study, little one!"

Thembi is only allowed her phone back to speak to her parents. It is easy for Shorty to put order in the room. She has captained the national side before, so captaining a matric student is a breezy task for her. Thembi's life runs according to Shorty's clock. She is up early, goes to bed early, drinks lots of water and – of course – studies. Shorty understands that the academic odds are really against Thembi here. With every second of daylight that passes, with every kick of the ball while Thembi is here, her peers are in class gaining an edge. Shorty exudes sternness and kindness in equal measure. Whenever she sees Thembi visibly struggling with her work, she approaches her, "If you don't understand something, don't be afraid. Ask me. If I don't know, we find out together. We ask your teachers, we ask the other ladies. There is always a way."

Shorty and Thembi spend hours poring over textbooks in between practices. Shorty watches Thembi closely. She takes notes on her attitude and is quick to slip advice into her ear.

"Shorty, I'm worried about Zulu. I wasn't speaking isiZulu growing up in Mohlakeng. I'm doomed."

Shorty takes Thembi by the arm and marches her down the hall, stopping at a room just before the staircase and knocking on the door.

"Who is it?"

Thembi and Shorty peep inside. Amanda Dlamini is relaxing on her bed, listening to music and chewing gum. At any point in time, Amanda is usually the coolest person in the room. Born in KwaZulu-Natal, she is an incredibly lethal footballer, but more than that, her swagger is intimidating.

"We need your help, Amanda."

"With what?"

"Thembi needs help passing isiZulu matric."

"I'm not a teacher."

"No, but you're a Zulu."

Amanda lets out a little chuckle, "I suppose you're right. Ngena phakhathi, uhlale phansi ngizokufundisa," she says, beckoning Thembi to sit down so she can teach her.

Shorty also nicknames Thembi "Madlanduna", because she

never stops eating. Night or day, rain or sunshine, Thembi can often be seen with a snack in hand. The input of food definitely does not match the output of her small frame.

"I will not let you fail just because you think you are going to make it in football," Shorty promises.

Shorty has far-reaching wisdom. She knows that even at this stage, where you are representing your national team as a woman footballer, you are far from guaranteed a career, let alone a living. For a South African woman, it is not a choice between football and education. It is both – or neither.

In addition to Thembi being commandeered by Shorty like a soldier, she is being closely monitored by Vera Pauw. Of course, it is not in the international coach's job description to be helping with schoolwork, but she does it gladly, if sternly. All of Thembi's work is sent to Vera, as well as her exam timetable, so that Vera can incorporate it into the training schedule.

It is not just watching soapies that Thembi misses out on due to geography and mathematics. One day, Banyana Banyana are in camp in Moruleng in the North West province. The national team is due to play Ivory Coast in an international friendly. There are two weeks to go before Vera selects her final 23 players for the upcoming AWCON in October. The players are granted a day off. There are two trips leaving today. The first is in the morning, to the mall. Here the girls can stock up on toiletries, snacks and anything else they may need. The second trip is to Sun City, the capital of the South African theme park scene, complete with waterslides, rollercoasters and a casino. It is undoubtedly more exhilarating than going to the mall. Most girls are in for both trips. However, Thembi is given a tough choice: "You can go to the mall, or you can go to Sun City, but you can't do both. You have an exam at 5pm today. If you choose to go to Sun City, I hope you do it with a good conscience."

Around the time Shorty, Amanda and the other players ride down the Boomerango slide, Thembi sharpens her pencil and takes her seat in an empty hall. When Thembi has to write an exam, it is Vera who is tasked with being her invigilator. No favours are given because of the coach-player relationship. Vera treats Thembi like a complete stranger when it comes to her writing exams. She slowly paces up and down the hall, with one eye trained on Thembi and the other fixed on her stopwatch. Thembi cannot help but give a little chuckle at the sight of Vera putting on her principal shoes – the role suits her well.

As the camp tour to Zimbabwe and Zambia approaches, the mentors in Thembi's life grow nervous. The camp is directly before one of her final exams. Her school principal, Granny and Thembi's parents are all in agreement that, although playing for the national team is a great honour, Thembi's academic future is more important. They want her to come home. Thembi realises she is going to need a good plea in order to sway those who care about her most.

"Just give me this one opportunity. Please. Just this once. Let me go on this camp. If I fail, let me fail. If it does not work out, I will come back, and I will put my everything into my academics."

"And what if you *do* make it as a footballer?"

"Then I will still put my everything into learning."

Thembi boards the flight to Zimbabwe. The players are beginning to gel and show their potential to play lethal football. They dominate the dry fields of Zimbabwe and then hop over the border to Zambia, where the trees are lush and the people are friendly – Banyana Banyana dominate there too. It is a gruelling, challenging and energy-sapping camp. The team is due to fly back to Johannesburg on a Monday. However, Thembi has her final geography exam on Monday. Arrangements are made, and tickets are shifted, and Thembi finds herself flying home by herself. On Sunday morning she wears the national jersey, scores goals and feels like a superhero. The next day she finds herself in a school uniform, writing down her exam number on the answer sheet, like every other learner out there.

CHAPTER 17

Not Good Enough

The national matric results come out in early January every year. Most people scour the newspaper until they see a name they recognise. It is not uncommon for newspapers to sell out on this day.

Thembi's father is awake at 3am. He puts on his coat and runs out in the rain to the newspaper seller down the road. Thembi's mother sits on the edge of the bed and nervously listens to her husband dodging puddles down the road.

"Wake up, Thembi. It's time to see whether you worked hard or not."

Thembi is still rubbing sleep from her eyes, shivering from the cold and contemplating the torture of being up before the sun when she hears her father. She can hear him long before she can see him. He is screaming, shouting, calling out inaudible cheers. He bursts into the room. He has the newspaper tightly gripped in one hand and is waving it around.

"You did it, Thembi! You did it!"

All in all, Thembi secures two distinctions, including an A for isiZulu. *Imagine. Me? Getting an A for Zulu? Ah, com'on man, you must be joking. I have Amanda Dlamini to thank for that. And I don't know if I ever told Shorty, but I owe my matric to her and all the things she did for me. The day I got my results, that was the happiest I had ever seen my father.*

Thembi's mother feels a celebration is in order and a feast will be cooked. *It was like Christmas that day. My mother cooked so much food. It was just me, my brothers and my parents. We ate until our stomachs could take no more, and we listened to music and danced until we slept – I saw how much education means to a family like mine. It was a good day.*

The smile does not fade from Thembi's father's face for days after the results come out. Pride thumps out of every one of his footsteps as he stops every person who crosses his path to tell them that his daughter has passed matric. He even drives Thembi all the way to Pretoria to fetch the official certificate. The whole of Mohlakeng is now familiar with Thembi's matric results. After that day Thembi is most looking forward to spending a bit of time closer to her family after the years in boarding school. It is for this reason that she applies at the Tshwane University of Technology (TUT).

All the way in Cape Town, around the time that Thembi has printed and filled out the last form on the application, there is a man throwing a bucket of human waste at a statue of the coloniser Cecil John Rhodes. As Thembi walks through the main entrance of TUT, she is unaware of how that seemingly small event in Cape Town is about to shape her future.

The statue in Cape Town gets defaced several more times in the next few days. The statue is eventually taken down, but the scars of what it represents remain. At the same time, it is announced that there will be an 11 per cent increase in university fees across the whole country. Universities all across the nation rise in protest, most of it peaceful. For 11 days, the country is gripped by a groundswell of powerful youthful revolutionary spirit known as Fees Must Fall. The movement sees students marching and singing at every university until the government announces a zero per cent increase in tuition fees.

Some protests run hotter than others, and during one particularly tense afternoon protest on the TUT campus, an administrative building is set on fire. A group of students, journalists and police watch from the outside as the bricks burn, the furniture sizzles, the windows explode, and Thembi's application to TUT disappears in the flames, a sacrifice to the revolution.

The University of the Western Cape (UWC) was founded around the year 1959. It has a history of standing firm against oppression, developing strong leaders and having its ear close to the South African ground. It is perhaps for this reason that it is the first university to hear that Thembi Kgatlana has no institution to score goals for this coming year. They send a representative to speak to the Kgatlana family.

"We think Thembi is the next big thing. We would love for her to study with us."

"Where?"

"In Cape Town."

Thembi shouts out from the corner of the room, "Cape Town! Damn, that's far." Thembi pictured herself being closer to family this year.

"We'll sort out everything. You don't have to do anything."

"Everything?"

"Everything."

Thembi goes to her cupboard and begins to pack her bags once again. She wonders what the weather in Cape Town is like. She packs extra socks just in case.

At first, university is challenging in a different kind of way. There is almost an overdose of freedom. At the HPC, there was a bell to wake you, a bell to tell you when to eat. A bell to tell you when to play and another one to tell you when to sleep. Even if the bell were to be dismantled, there was no shortage of mentors keeping an eagle eye on Thembi. At university, Thembi finds herself free to do as she pleases. Whether she goes to lectures, sleeps in or eats badly is completely up to her. But the consequences of ill discipline are so long term that Thembi's own conscience is her referee.

Thembi is enrolled for a bachelor's degree in tourism. The university places her in a decent residence and ensures she has everything she might need to graduate. The university is a grand institution, with great white pillars and a red chapel pointing to the sky. Thembi is in awe the first time she sees it. She remains in awe.

The buildings give her a profound sense of hope and opportunity.

Once again, Thembi finds herself with heavier shoulders than her peers. The balance between studying, enjoying a social life and representing the national team is one that requires intense discipline. Luckily for Thembi, she meets a man at UWC who is on a mission to keep her humble.

Sanele is commonly known as Saider. He runs Thembi through her extra training sessions. He works her like she owes him a debt. No matter the weather, which can be volatile at best in the Cape, Saider has Thembi running laps and dodging cones until her legs collapse. Thembi brings her footballing ferocity to the university fields and regularly dominates the weekend fixtures. However, Saider, much like Thembi's father, is not too fond of compliments, and rarely gives credit, not even where it is needed. It is not uncommon for Thembi to score multiple goals on the weekend, only for Saider to just keep quiet when she returns to training on Monday. She knows he saw the game, but he pretends as if she has just returned from doing something completely unspectacular, like drying her laundry.

One day, fed up with the lack of reinforcement from Saider, Thembi goes into destruction mode during a game. She does not stop running until all of her opponents are bent over with their hands on their knees, deeply sucking in air. Every time Thembi has the ball, she passes at least three defenders. Every time she does not have the ball, she shouts until it is passed back. She does not stop scoring until she has buried five into the back of the net, and the referee mercifully blows his whistle to allow the other team to exit the slaughterhouse.

Thembi arrives at training the next day with a particular bounce in her step. Saider is already on the field, methodically placing orange cones. Thembi jogs right up to him, stares into his face and smiles. Saider does not look at her; he just continues placing cones, one after the other.

"Well?"

"Well?"

"Aren't you going to say something?"

"About what?"

"About my game."

"What about your game?"

"I don't know, Sanele, how about the fact that I scored five goals? How about the fact that this whole university cannot stop saying my name after that last match, but for some reason you won't say anything – not a word."

Saider briefly pauses his cone placing, looks at Thembi from the side of his eye, and smiles at her with the side of his mouth.

"And still you say nothing?"

"What is it you want me to say?"

"How about, 'Good game, Thembi. Well played, Thembi. You are really improving, Thembi'?"

Saider drops the remaining cones. He turns to face Thembi and lets out a sigh that whistles with disappointment.

"You want a compliment for that? You want a compliment for scoring five goals against the weakest team in the league? Nah man, my grandmother could have scored five goals against those girls. You see, that's the problem here. You are too happy to celebrate these small victories. What happens when you play a serious women's side? Imagine, one day, you will have to play against China, against the USA. Against girls who have been training in academies their whole lives, who eat right and have mentors – girls who were born for this. How are you preparing for that? How are you going to defeat the giants? You're not going to do it by practising against mice."

The words sting Thembi's ears, but she knows that as harsh as they are, they are true.

Saider is not the only one who trains Thembi, and she makes an impression on all her coaches. UWC head coach Nathan Peskin remembers being struck by Thembi's confidence in every situation: "I remember one day we went for a warm-up run. At the end of this run was a market where they were selling a beautiful necklace. Thembi could see me looking at this necklace and asked if I liked it. I said I did but that it was too expensive. Best believe little Thembi stood there and bargained down the price for her coach until I could afford it."

When the 2015 Varsity Cup rolls around, Thembi is in better shape than ever due to Saider's regime. The first game is under the spotlights of the UWC stadium. There is a buzzing crowd to welcome Tuks from Tshwane as they come to battle Thembi and the UWC girls. Thembi can hear the crowd from inside the changeroom. She feels a ball of emotion swirling around in her throat, but she keeps a cool face. She emerges from the room and into the hallway. A pair of short arms wrap around her and squeeze her tight. Thembi turns around to see a smiling Simphiwe Shorty Dludlu. She is the coach of Tuks today and jokes with Thembi that UWC are doomed. Thembi feels her nerves calm. Even though Shorty is the opposing coach, her face is always a welcome sight. They wish each other luck and walk in separate directions onto the field. One of the assistant coaches of Tuks then walks just behind Thembi and says something under her breath, audible but muffled, "Hey, Thembi Kgatlana, this isn't Jo'burg, you hear me? You can't just run circles around the girls here. You can't just go off and score five goals. And if you think you can, ha! You'll see. You'll get kicked like you've never been kicked before."

Unaware of the error she just made, the coach walks away before Thembi can reply and joins Shorty and the rest of her team. *When you provoke me, you make a mistake, because I'll make you swallow your words, and then you won't know what to do next.*

The first half ignites with Thembi breaking early, getting past three defenders and narrowly missing the goal. As she is jogging back, she hears Shorty shouting to her team, "Stay on Thembi! If the midfield breaks and passes the ball to her, that ball will be in the back of the net. Mark my words, don't give her an inch to breathe."

Shorty has barely finished her last words when Thembi intercepts a high ball, brings it down with the deftness of a leopard, scrapes the ball with the outside of her boot, looks up momentarily and then fires a comet past the keeper and into the net. The stadium erupts, Thembi springs up and punches the air, it's 1-0 to UWC. The elation from the goal blurs the focus of UWC, and a couple lousy missed tackles leads to an easy equaliser for Tuks, 1-1. Now it's all-out war. The atmosphere thickens by the second, and the match gets more physical. Player to player, boot to boot, no player hesitates in any collision. Thembi's courage grows as she sees the ball bounce over a defender, opening a window for her to slip through towards the goal. She can picture the ball in the back of the net already. As Thembi recoils her right foot in preparation for the shot, her world goes black. She feels pain in all corners of her body, and when she opens her eyes again, a defender twice Thembi's size is peeling her body off of Thembi's. Thembi shakes her head, blinks hard and tries to stand, only to find that she cannot. She looks down at her knee and winces. She waves her hand in the air and points at her knee until the paramedics slide in to attend to her. The UWC players wear worry on their face like a mask.

"Come on Thembi! Walk it off! We need you."

"No. No. No! She needs an ambulance," shouts Shorty in protest.

"She's in bad shape. Get her to the hospital," the Tuks players agree.

The medics prod and rub and spray Thembi's knee, but they still shake their heads: "It really doesn't look good."

Thembi lies back on the grass and takes a moment to see the world upside down. She looks around at the packed stadium, the desperation on the faces of her teammates and the hope on the faces of her enemy. She sits back up, grabs the medic's shirt and pulls him closer.

"Listen here, Doc, I'm going back onto that field. I'm not leaving my teammates out there to battle alone. This knee, the one that's chilling on the side of my leg right now, you're going to pop it back into place. Do what you gotta do, so I can do what I gotta do."

Thembi puts her head back on the grass and clenches her teeth as the medic twists, pulls and pops Thembi's knee back into shape and she re-joins her team to secure the victory.

UWC goes on to have a fantastic tournament. They reach the

final, where they come up against TUT, the university that would have had Thembi Kgatlana on their team had their administration building not been torched. Thembi is still limping, hobbling off the same injury that struck her in the opening game of the tournament. Regardless of the pain though, she plays on. Not only does she play on, she plays as if the game of football is going to cease to exist tomorrow. The game fires with entertainment value, both teams showing the mettle of champions. Thembi scores a phenomenal goal. Unfortunately for her team though, her goal is a solitary one for UWC, and they walk away with the silver medal at the end of the day. Even though Thembi is on the losing side, she is still awarded the Woman of the Match award, an impressive accolade for a player representing the defeated side.

Thembi hardly notices her accolade though. She takes the loss personally. The silver medal around her neck feels more like an insult than a merit. She wears disappointment on her chin when she shows up to training the next day. She is quiet, waiting for Saider's morning criticism. She braces for it like one does for an expected slap. Saider looks Thembi up and down and then says something soft, but powerful, before jogging off as if he never said it at all: "You know, Thembi, sometimes winning is not about being victorious. Sometimes winning is just about you. Sometimes, we want to win so badly that we become blind to the things that make us champions every day."

CHAPTER 18

Portia Has Left the Building

After a season of dominance, those closest to Thembi fear that she is not being tested enough, and that she will be doomed to a career of mediocrity unless something can be done about it.

Vera Pauw tasks her assistant coach and Banyana Banyana legend Desiree Ellis with solving the matter. Desiree organises for Thembi to train with the boys at Ajax Cape Town. Desiree and Vera think this will give Thembi the edge and toughness she will need if Banyana Banyana are to stand any chance against the more physical teams on the continent. The World Cup qualifiers loom, and South Africa has never managed to book a spot in the biggest sporting tournament in the world before.

Joining Ajax CT was a very jarring experience for Thembi. She has always assumed that the elements involved in boys' football were more luxurious than for girls, but now she sees it first-hand. The players have access to the best food, the leanest nutritionists, the firmest physios and the shrewdest tacticians. The coaching staff are surprised and impressed by Thembi's ability to tussle with the men on the team, and they do a good job of toughening her up even more before the qualifiers begin.

The first qualifier is against Kenya, and only minutes into the game, Thembi suffers a bad injury. She can feel it is more than a tweaked muscle. Her stomach sinks at the thought of Banyana

Banyana watching another World Cup on TV and knowing she could not fight for them to be there.

Thembi undergoes intensive healing and rehabilitation. She watches week after week as Banyana Banyana fly through the qualifiers and dismantle their opponents one by one while yet another girl wears Thembi's jersey. Thembi has to start from the beginning again, basic and frustrating exercises, nothing too intense so as not to inflame her injury. The patience required feels like poison to Thembi. When she flicks on the TV and watches Janine lead the troops out to battle, she can almost hear what the captain is saying. She can almost feel the vibration of the stadium under her feet. When a ball is crossed into the box, Thembi kicks out her right leg instinctively, forgetting for a moment that she is not on the field.

As Thembi is recovering from her injury, she joins the players in camp as they prepare for their international friendly against Cameroon. When the players wake up in the morning, the sky is dark, streaming an ominous message, and the clouds look heavily pregnant with bad news. Training is delayed despite all the players being dressed and on the field in time. Vera is in the corner talking to Portia Modise. Both women look distressed, pleading with each other, shaking their heads and waving their hands. When Portia re-joins the team for the warm-up, she whispers under her breath, "There is going to be a press conference later on today. I just want you all to be prepared."

It feels like a death in the family when Portia announces her retirement from international football. *We were devastated. We really thought Portia would play forever.* Thembi had lain awake many nights, picturing Portia and herself, with arms around each other, celebrating a goal that they just masterfully crafted, running to go celebrate with fans waving the South African flag. Those dreams would now have to be parked in the fantasy bay forever. There is one positive to the news though – there is a massive hole in the striker department of the national team up for the taking.

CHAPTER 19

Operation Rio de Janeiro

In 2016, Thembi makes an unbreakable promise to herself: no matter what, she *will* make it. She has to make it, or settle into a life of obscurity. A woman footballer needs to be constantly working on her body and her mind if she is to make it. Thembi is a lover of books. She devours history and thirsts for learning about different cultures. She remembers reading books about the Olympics, and the original Olympians, how they stood tall above the rest of humankind, and used their superior skill and strength to conquer the world. Thembi draws a line in her mind from those original men in Ancient Greece, to 2008 and Usain Bolt officially becoming the fastest person to ever live. She carries on drawing that line in her mind until she arrives at a picture of herself, her shoulders wrapped in green and gold, a flag in her hands. She hears the roar of the stadium and sees the South African flag hanging from the ceiling. She sees herself as the modern Olympian, and she knows that she has to do whatever it takes to get there.

Not everything is in her control though. Vera Pauw is studying her team sheet like a scientist in a lab. She knows she has to get the balance right. Too many young players in the team, and the occasion might just overwhelm them. Their hopes will be crushed. However, too many old players in the team is also risky; every now and then there is a moment on the field, where an experienced cool head decides to go for caution, when really what the situation requires is a bit of fire.

After a long series of trials, trainings and matches, all the players are released to go home and breathe. Thembi loves going home. Not a whole lot changes on Mohapi Street. When Thembi walks around with her friends and greets elders, she feels 13 again. Only one thing changes when Thembi Kgatlana goes back to Mohlakeng – she is a little more famous every time, and her community is a little prouder of her.

In this rare moment of no football, Thembi takes her time and sleeps in. She has a slow, smooth and complete breakfast, and then she heads out the door onto Mohapi Street. Thembi is content with how her day ahead is looking. She is on her way to her friend's house, they plan to jam some PlayStation, go to the mall and spend the day laughing at one another. *But then I got this feeling. It was not a good feeling or a bad feeling, but it was there and it let me know something was coming.* Thembi's pocket vibrates. Her Nikes stop in their step. She reaches into her pocket. It's Vera Pauw. As she's about to swipe, she freezes. Thembi cannot remember the last time she breathed. Ten seconds pass, her life story flashes before her mind's eye, and she still cannot seem to find the strength to answer. She blinks hard, snaps out of it and slides her thumb across the screen.

"Hello, Vera?"

"Hello Thembi, I am calling you to talk about the Olympics."

"Ah, yes, Vera, I'm fine thanks."

"Listen Thembi, you are still very young."

Thembi hears a distant crack, like the legs of the chair she is sitting on are about to collapse, and there is not a thing she can do about it.

"Thembi, you have worked so hard this year. We have noticed it, but still, you are very young."

"So I'm not in the squad?"

"Thembi, you did not make the 18-woman squad that will be starting off in Brazil."

Thembi fights back the tears, "Okay, thank you, Coach."

"I'm not finished talking, Thembi.

"Okay Coach..."

"We are allowed to take three extra players and a goalkeeper, in case of injury or something like that. This means that we have 22 tickets for players going to Brazil."

"Okay Coach, and...?"

"And? And you now have to go check if your passport is good and come fetch your ticket to Rio de Janeiro from me. You're going to be an Olympian, Thembi."

Thembi only breathes again after the call is finished. Within half an hour, the whole of Mohlakeng knows that one of their own is going to the Olympics.

AS THE PLANE DESCENDS INTO Guarulhos International Airport, the lush greenery of Brazil reaches up and grabs one in one's seat and pulls one down into its humid belly. The air in Brazil slaps with rhythm, style and smoothness. Thembi feels at home as soon as she steps off the plane. *I was in a really humble space when we landed in Brazil. I was not under the pressure of being in the first team, and I could just enjoy the place. I love travelling, and I love nature, and football has given me the keys to a lot of natural beauty around the world.*

On the day off, most of the other Banyana Banyana players want to go to the famous beaches of Rio de Janeiro, to see the coconuts and bikinis and buy silky scarves for back home. Thembi does not join them. She has a different kind of mission. During the previous days' training, something she saw in the distance kept on bugging her. It stood upon a mountain in the distance, towering over the entire bay of Rio. Sometimes the clouds hid it, but Thembi always felt its shadow. She knew that her first glimpse of time off would be spent trying to get closer to the statue.

On the day, Thembi and two other teammates wake before the sun and take the cart all the way to the top of Mount Corcovado. The statue of Christ the Redeemer is difficult to behold. It is massive, but to get a picture with the statue is challenging, as the weather changes by the minute at such high altitude. Adding to the challenge is the fact that Thembi and her teammates are not the only ones coming to see the monument. Thembi laughs uncontrollably as they try to estimate the right spot to be in to get the perfect picture in the rare moments that the clouds release the statue. If they get their position wrong, when the clouds clear, there will be a thousand people between Thembi and Christ the Redeemer, and the picture will be spoiled.

The Olympic Village for the athletes is undoubtedly the most well-thought-out space Thembi has ever been in her life. There is every attention to detail. Every convenience one could conceive of is there. Everything is within arm's reach, and everything is free. There is a salon where players can get their hair done before a big event. There is a McDonald's in the Village where you can go grab two burgers and a pack of fries before changing your mind about the first burger. There are charging ports on every corner, and the walls are lined with bright red refrigerators, brimming with cans of Coca-Cola. Thembi also receives a new smartphone on arrival; all the athletes do. Samsung has brought out a limited edition device especially for the Olympians; the buttons are painted in the Olympic colours.

There is one thing that makes Thembi realise she is in the Olympic Village more than anything else, and that is the sight of a giant walking towards her. His head is high, his shoulders are back and his face is relaxed. He walks with the stride of the king of the jungle. Thembi only needs a silhouette to know that it is Usain Bolt. She feels the magnetic presence of greatness and pauses to appreciate it. He flashes Thembi a smile before cruising onwards. Thembi and her teammates see him a number of other times around the Village. It is difficult for him to conceal his identity, and he can barely place three steps without someone asking him to pose with them. One day, Thembi sees him exiting the dining hall. He's still wiping his mouth after his meal and probably thinking about the podium he is going to be standing on later. A number of athletes walk towards him with their cameras and pens extended. But he's in no mood for autographs today, so takes off, in his familiar sprint, down the hallway with an excited crowd of gushing Olympic athletes in tow. These are the Olympic moments that happen away from the camera.

The only time the smile dissolves from Thembi's face is when the team hits the field. It is only their second ever Olympics, and Banyana Banyana are undoubtedly poised to be mice in a group of lionesses. Before the tournament starts, all the teams get a warm-up game against a team not in their group. Banyana Banyana play New Zealand. She's not in the squad for this match, so Thembi watches from the stands among the other fans. She and the reserves grimace and wince as a nightmare unfolds before their eyes. South Africa find themselves on the hammer's end of a 5-1 drubbing. They go back to the Village to lick their wounds.

South Africa's first official game is against Sweden. Right at the death of the match, one of the South African strikers slams into a brutal collision with an opposing player. She goes down and does not come up again until a stretcher carries her off the field. After the game, the physio informs Vera that she will need to find a new striker before the next game. Vera summons Thembi to her room that night. She says few words, letting the occasion fill the silence in the room. She asks Thembi if she is ready, but she already knows Thembi's answer from the moment she looks in her eyes.

Banyana Banyana's second game is against China, a powerhouse in women's football. Thembi feels as though she only snaps into consciousness when she is standing on the field. She looks around at the manicured grass under her boots, the sharp lights beaming off the top of this state-of-the-art stadium, the heaving fans. She is 20 years old. A few moments ago she was a spectator, and as soon as the whistle blows and Thembi starts running, she knows she is now an Olympian.

Banyana Banyana battle out a fierce game of football against China. Thembi has a locked grip on the throttle, getting in behind the Chinese defenders and wowing the international spectators with a level of skill, pace and flair that they have never quite seen before. Opposition fans delight in watching Thembi with the ball and even applaud as she terrorises their own defenders. Despite the spirited attacking game, Banyana Banyana lose the game 2-0 and are given little time to mourn before the next clash.

The day after the China game, Vera does something unusual. Instead of going on to the usual training session, she calls the Banyana Banyana players to a meeting in a conference room. She tells everyone to settle down as she dims the lights and fiddles with a screen at the front of the room. She turns to face the national team.

"Ladies, our next game is against Brazil. We are in Brazil. This is not a football-loving nation, Brazil *is* football. When you walk out into the Maracanã tomorrow, it will be unlike anything you have experienced in your life. None of you have ever played in front of 100 000 people before. The noise will sting your ears. When they play the national anthem, you will be trembling. You will stop thinking about football. You will be so caught up in the intensity of it all that you will forget what position you are playing. Your mind will be taken out of the game and before you have even realised you are playing, you will be two goals down. This is serious."

Vera hits a button and plays a clip of the Brazilian national team singing their anthem.

"We are going to feel nervous tomorrow," Vera continues. "We are going to work out our nerves here, so that we can focus on the game tomorrow. I'm assuming you've heard of Marta?"

Thembi describes Marta Vieira da Silva as the "goddess of football". She is the all-time top scorer in the World Cup. She has been voted as the FIFA Women's Player of the Year six times, five of them in a row. More importantly, she is the first human of any gender to score in five different World Cups, spanning over two decades. On the streets, in the stadium, in the Village, everyone has Marta-10 on their backs. Tomorrow, Thembi Kgatlana, the little girl from Mohlakeng, will go toe to toe with the great Marta.

The Maracanã can be viewed as a religious monument of football. Before it had seats installed, it is said to have welcomed standing crowds of up to 200 000 people to its games. Historic moments have gone down in this stadium, collective national joy and pain all focused around one patch of grass. From the South African changeroom, the noise of the stadium sounds like distant thunder, rolling in a storm over the mountains. Generous predictions forecast Banyana Banyana getting drilled by at least five or six goals. But South Africa as a nation has an incredible capacity to stand fearless against dark odds. The national women's football team is the embodiment of that spirit, for few athletes have had to overcome odds so unfavourable as the 18 South African women sitting in an Olympic changeroom in the Maracanã that day. South Africa has always found its courage for battle through song, and so the rhythmic sounds of studs tapping against a concrete floor begin to echo off the corners of the changeroom. Thembi sings: "Amahlathi aphelile, akusekho ukucasha!" (There is no time to hide in the forest, it's time for war).

The rest of the team follow: "Amahlathi aphelile, akusekho ukucasha!"

They stand and they clap and they dance in circles, summoning more courage. Janine leads them out of the changeroom and into the tunnel. They are ready. Banyana Banyana stand strong and united, stone-faced as they patiently wait out the roar of the Brazilian national anthem. Little is said in the team huddle. The diamond-sharp focus can be felt and seen on the face of every South African player. The referee blows the whistle to start the game; it sounds to Thembi like the door of a cage swinging open, and she is the untamed tiger inside.

South Africa makes sure to disrupt Brazil's every movement, following their opposition like a shadow and sticking right under their feet – Brazil can barely get a pass away. The stadium becomes more tense as the game winds on; the anxiety of the fans adds to the atmosphere. Marta can feel the pressure of her nation's desperation to avoid Olympic heartbreak today. Marta kicks into the next gear and tries to weave her way through the South African defence, dazzling with the ball and sending other players off on runs. Every time Marta finds a space though, she is met with a bone-crunching, momentum-killing challenge. On the other end, Thembi is wearing the Brazilian defenders down, jogging in circular patterns around them before exploding off in a ferocious sprint towards the goal.

When the referee blows the final whistle, some Brazilian players drop to their knees and others fall to their back; they are spent. South Africa has held the hosts to a goalless draw. It is not a victory for either team in the strict sense of the word, but it is undoubtedly a monumental moral triumph for Banyana Banyana. In the changeroom after the game, Vera wears an expression she has never worn before – something beyond pride. She addresses her team: "I want you ladies to always remember this moment. No matter where you go from here in life, always be proud of yourself for this moment. You matched the world's greatest today. There were almost 100 000 people in that stadium today, and not a single one of them was supporting you, but you still rose up and did what you had to do."

CHAPTER 20

Are You Even a Part of This Team?

After the last game at the 2016 Olympics, Vera Pauw gathers all the players and tells them that she has run her course as captain of the ship. She wishes them the best and thanks them for the memories.

When Thembi returns from the Olympics, there are many things on her mind and in her heart, and studying is not at the top of her list. Her parents and other mentors encourage her to return to UWC and finish her second year of studying. Thembi spends a long time taking stock of her life and the paths laid out before her, and much to the disappointment of several people, she decides to suspend her studies.

These are just some of the tough decisions that you have to take in life. At some point, if being successful is in your plans, you're going to have to take some risk. Yes, school is important, it always will be, but nowadays, opportunities are more important than anything. How many people have degrees but no jobs? They're not working, because the opportunity is not always there – not because they did not go to school. It is opportunity that changes your life. I had an opportunity to become a professional footballer, and I knew the risks – if I got injured, I couldn't just pretend to be a professional footballer. I also knew that I could always go back to school at a later stage in life, but this opportunity would not always be here.

At the Olympics, Thembi had been exposed to a different kind of professionalism and it had given her a thirst for cementing herself in professional football structures. Whenever you see a South African footballer playing overseas, you must understand the footballing education that the player has had. Thembi, like thousands of other players in the country, grew up playing on a gravel pitch – bumpy, rocky and dusty. The ball moves at a different pace on a gravel pitch, allowing for very tricky and skilful play. The best and most skilful football in South Africa undoubtedly happens on gravel, unseen by most of the world. When transported to a perfectly manicured grass field, however, the style often gets lost in translation. Truly great players can blend the two styles and infuse a foreign team with local flavour – and Thembi wants to be one of the greats.

People who grow up playing on gravel fields will tell you how difficult it is to make the switch to grass. There is also grass that is well taken care of – and then there is ankle-destroying grass. Compared to the rest of Africa, South Africa's fields are great. So many teams want to come play in South Africa, trust me, but when they get here, they play on the nice grass and they lose focus. They want to go shopping and see all the other sites, and then they forget they have a game. We are a very skilful group of players, so the other African teams try to bully us. Ghana, Nigeria, Cameroon – they are all the same. They kick us and spit on us. They trip and they pinch and they pull our hair. We have had to become a mentally tough group of girls. But these things make you tough. In football and in life, people only try to kick you when you are playing well.

Thembi gets a lesson in toughness after Banyana Banyana land in Cameroon to take part in the 2016 AWCON. As luck would have it, South Africa are scheduled to play their first match against the hosts. The whole of Cameroon bands together to make South Africa feel as unwelcome as possible. From the hotel to the stadium they are met with hostility, dirty looks and aggressively pointed fingers. When the bus parks, there is an angry presence of heavily armed army forces to meet them at the stadium. The guards are

Are You Even a Part of This Team?

officially there for crowd control but unofficially, their job is to intimidate Banyana Banyana. The changing room is dark, dirty and reeks of freshly spilt urine.

The game itself is fiery. There are more bums than seats in the stadium. The roar of the Cameroonian spirit hits Thembi like a slap to the ear as she exits the tunnel. She tries to get into her groove, play her usual game, use her speed to cause havoc. However, the Cameroonian defenders have her number. They are giants, strong, athletic and unforgiving. They bounce Thembi between their shoulders, chip away at her ankles and make sure that she cannot get a spot of space on the field. The referee blows the halftime whistle; the scores are locked at zero apiece as the players jog off the field.

The changeroom is charged with emotion. The South African players know they are not playing their usual game; they cannot get any sort of momentum. They're nursing all kinds of bruises, scars and scratches. Assistant Coach Desiree Ellis has taken over the post left empty by Vera Pauw for now. Coach Des enters the changeroom last. Her anger and frustration is visible. Thembi almost feels as if steam is about to come streaming out of the coach's ears. As Coach Des enters the room, she drops her clipboard and shakes her head.

"Thembi! Linda! You are doing nothing out there! Your team needs you, and you are nowhere! Are you even a part of this team? Your country needs you, and you are nowhere to be found. Either make something happen, or both of you are on the bench for the rest of this tournament, because right now you two are doing absolutely nothing out there."

The words echo in Thembi's head: *You are doing nothing*. She goes to the bathroom. She needs a quiet moment to pull herself together. She tries to imagine how she will be better in the second half, how she could play more like herself, but all she can hear is *you are doing nothing*.

The players go out for the second half. Banyana Banyana have a renewed energy, but today Cameroon are a team possessed. For South Africa it feels like they are squaring up against a team of heavyweight boxers. About 10 minutes into the second half, Thembi tries to do a quick change of direction to chase a ball, and she is met with a solid six-studded boot to the chest. It sounds like a war drum as she goes flying backwards and sprawls out on the ground, seeing stars and spots. Coach Des takes Thembi off. She does not say anything.

Thembi does not play the next match, nor the match after that. And when South Africa line up against Ghana for their last game, Thembi is still scheduled to start on the bench. The game is indicative of South Africa's tournament in general. They fail to find their rhythm and generally look dazed and out of place. With 10 minutes to go, Ghana score and go through to the next round. Coach Des turns to look at Thembi for the first time since the first game in tournament, she nods her head towards the field. No words are used to tell Thembi that the team needs her again. As Thembi walks from the bench and onto the field, she feels something missing. An empty and dark space where her heart used to be. *You are doing nothing.* The words roll around her head like marbles in a glass jar. She cannot think of anything else. The referee blows the final whistle, and Thembi hardly realises that she has been in a game. Her body was there, but her mind was in the changeroom on that first day when they lost to the host country. South Africa board the flight back home in a sombre mood.

CHAPTER 21

Changing Momentum

Thembi, you are doing nothing. Thembi has had much time to contemplate the words. At first they hurt her, taking her to the depths of self-doubt. Thembi feels a great pain when she thinks of the failed expedition to Cameroon. But everybody has to leave the darkness at some point, so she looks ahead. She reasons that she still has breath in her body and blood in her legs; she still has an opportunity to pull it back.

In 2016, although no longer studying, Thembi is still playing for the UWC team in the Sasol Women's League. For a while, the best team in the region has been Cape Town Roses FC, a fierce squad from Gugulethu. In an away game to them, Thembi wreaks havoc on their defence, proving impossible to keep up with, finding energy from a bottomless well. After another zooming run, Thembi jogs back to her half when she hears the opposition coach yell out to her team while pointing at Thembi: "Why are you so scared of this one little girl? Just kick her. Kick her hard enough so that she goes down and gets out and is no longer our problem."

For the rest of the game, Thembi takes one – no, two, even three – for the team. She grinds through every ankle-splitting slide tackle, every elbow to the temple and every knee to the calf. She largely absorbs the abuse and creates space for the rest of her team. UWC emerge victorious and qualify for the final of the championship.

The winner of the next game is the undisputed best women's

football team in the country. They are due to face an interesting team owned by Banyana Banyana captain Janine van Wyk, named JVW FC. It is a particularly feared team, as about eight players in JVW FC also feature in the starting line-up of Banyana Banyana.

UWC may have Thembi Kgatlana, but they also have players who, mere months before, had only ever seen these Banyana Banyana heroines on television. Today they face them as opponents. The JVW players who are their opponents today. Many of the UWC players are starstruck – Thembi can sense it. It is the way they say Amanda, Janine and Linda's names. She knows that her teammates are thinking more about meeting their opponents than beating them.

The UWC team huddles before the game, with all the coaching and medical staff. Thembi can see the players looking over their shoulders, watching Amanda Dlamini warm up and becoming visibly more nervous. Thembi senses that the occasion requires someone to step up and lead. Her voice booms through the middle of the circle. She asks everyone who is not in the starting line-up to please leave the circle. The coaches and extended staff grumble and sulk off back towards the bench. Thembi addresses her troops: "If you want to idolise Amanda, do it after the game! Approach her in the hotel or in the changeroom, but do not idolise her here! In the game, there is no difference between you and Amanda. She is playing, you are also playing. She has two feet, you also have two feet. You both are playing with the exact same opportunity to win. We have to focus today. Everything we do today, we're going to do like it's the last game of our lives. There is no tomorrow – we leave it all on the field today."

The game starts, the atmosphere is emotional. The tackles are especially physical from the get-go, and around 10 minutes in, Linda Motlhalo weaves a dazzling run into the box. A UWC defender throws herself at Linda's leg like a grenade. Linda comes crashing down in front of the goal and the referee blows for a penalty. Thembi is furious. The required intensity is there, but the discipline is not, and now they find themselves down 1-0.

To Thembi's surprise, JVW FC place an unusual defender to

mark her – a meek, scrawny white girl lacking in both pace and skill – yet the look on her face says that she feels fairly confident about her chances against Thembi today. Thembi bounces lightly on her toes from foot to foot. Letting a subtle smile creep across her face, she knows she is about to make breakfast out of this defender.

As soon as play restarts, Thembi cranks up the voltage, sprinting off and jogging backwards, testing and checking her opponent. Thembi receives the ball on the wing. She rounds her right foot over it and then pushes the ball through her opponent's legs with her left foot. She runs around the defender, collects the ball on the other side and hits a low, hard shot into the bottom corner of the goal. The game is tied at 1-1.

Thembi terrorises her opposite number for another 20 minutes. The white defender has now turned pink as she tries to play through desperate gasps of air. Her hands are on her knees, her head is facing the ground, and her legs are shot. Thembi is just getting started, barely breaking a bead of sweat. The coach of JVW FC makes the correct and long overdue decision of substituting the defender.

The break in play switches momentum, and soon JVW FC are back ahead 2-1. Thembi takes a deep breath. She knows her work is far from over. She sets off again. Her Banyana Banyana teammates can hardly believe the game she is playing. She has lightning in her legs, and she is controlling the ball like a puppet master. It seems inevitable when Thembi scores a cracker from the edge of the box to tie up the game at 2-2. Some of the JVW FC players even nod their heads in subtle approval of Thembi's latest strike. With 10 minutes to go, JVW FC summon all their experience and masterfully craft a set of intricate passes. The UWC players chase the ball like a child after a butterfly, but before long the ball is in their box, and with just one minute left on the clock, it ends up in the back of the net. JVW FC win the match 3-2, but the real highlight is the performance by Thembi Kgatlana, which earns her the Woman of the Match award.

CHAPTER 22

A Whack Left Foot

At the beginning of 2017, Thembi resumes her studies. She is now settled after the Olympics and the AWCON. Thembi kicks off the year with the good news that she has been chosen to represent South Africa at the Universiade, the world university games, in Taipei, the capital of Taiwan. Thembi meets up with the squad at OR Tambo International and chats excitedly with her new teammates. The coach of the national student team is Thinasonke Mbuli, and she is booked to sit next to Thembi on the flight on the way over.

A curious thing about Thembi Kgatlana is that she is a bubbly, smiling human most of the time, but when she is provoked – something ignites inside of her. When someone doubts her, the tiger in her soul awakes from its slumber. Whether Thinasonke Mbuli knows this when she talks to Thembi is unclear, but the coach is not afraid to speak her mind.

"Ja, you know, I saw your last game – the final against JVW. You are a good player, it would be impossible to say otherwise. But for me, a good player has to be complete, and there is definitely something that lacks within you."

Thinasonke straightens out the newspaper in front of her and starts skimming the headlines. Thembi looks at her in shock.

"Well, what is it that I lack?"

Thinasonke puts down the newspaper.

A Whack Left Foot

"Your left foot is whack. You need to sharpen it. I know, if ever I'm coaching a team that's playing against you, I will just tell my players to stick on your right and force you onto your left, easy as a Sunday."

The coach picks up the paper again, signalling the end of the conversation. Thembi stares at the seat in front of her, wearing a reflective, yet startled expression on her face. A few hours into the flight, Coach Thinasonke is sleeping. Thembi has not stopped thinking about her left foot. Thembi shakes her coach awake.

"Thembi? What is it?"

"Let's make a bet."

"What kind of bet?"

"For every goal I score off my left foot in this tournament, you have to give me $10."

The coach laughs, turns over and closes her eyes again before mumbling: "Very easy, Thembi. It will snow in Mohlakeng before you score a goal with your left foot."

In the first game against Great Britain, the ball gets played in just behind the British defenders; it bounces high and forward. Thembi tears down the wing like a Labrador after a stick. As the ball is halfway through its bounce, Thembi meets it with her left shoelaces mid-air. Like a heat-seeking missile, the ball whistles past the hapless British goalkeeper and detonates into the back of the net. It is always a sweet symbol of historical justice when a South African sports team levels a beating on their former colonial overseers, and the girls from down South serve it cold today. Thembi scores another goal – South Africa clobber the British 3-1.

The opening game has another consequence – something rewires in Thembi's legs. The cogs in her calves begin to turn, and her feet begin to do things they have never done before, scoring goals they have never scored before. South Africa beats the USA 1-0 in the next game.

As South Africa dislodge opponent after opponent and they progress further in the tournament, it seems as if they may just get their first ever Universiade medal. In the playoff games, South Africa comes up against Russia, and something bizarre happens with the weather. The first half of the game happens in the calm before the storm; the air is humid and sticky, heavy and hot. The South African girls relish the heat, running diagonals through their breathless, pink-faced Russian opponents. Thembi especially is having fun, mocking the defenders with every sly movement of the ball. When the referee blows for halftime, South Africa are 1-0 ahead.

During the break, the storm rolls in. The stadium goes dark, and the temperature halves. The South Africans freeze up, and the Russians come to life, sneaking in an impressive five-goal comeback. The South African team goes home in a darkened mood, but on the flight home, Thembi is wide awake, her eyes looking through the plane's front windscreen, to her destiny ahead. She knows she has found a rhythm and is about to unleash some potent football into the world.

THE COUNCIL OF SOUTHERN African Football Associations (COSAFA) Cup is a competition between a number of Southern African national teams. This year's tournament is in Zimbabwe, during the sizzling month of September. Desiree Ellis has officially been announced as the Banyana Banyana coach. She is a legend of the local game, having scored a hattrick in South Africa's first ever international game, against Swaziland (later eSwatini), making a massive contribution to her country's 14-0 demolition job victory. There is hardly a woman in the land more deserving of the top coaching honour in the country.

Desiree can see a newly lit fire in Thembi's eyes when she reports for COSAFA duty, but she also still sees a young player needing time to grow. She seats Thembi on the bench for the first game against Lesotho. With the scores gridlocked at 0-0, Thembi is brought on. With her first touch of the ball she rounds a defender; with her next touch, she passes a sweet assist to her teammate for the opening goal. A few touches after that, and Thembi scores a thunderous goal to help South Africa win 3-1.

In the next game against Namibia, Thembi bangs in two more goals at either end of the game to secure another victory. In the semifinals, South Africa come up against Zambia. Never in the history of women's football has Zambia beaten South Africa, yet on this day their chances sparkle brighter than usual. They have a steady, thick stream of support behind them and an uncharacteristically strong team. Zambia's momentum becomes very real when they score two quick goals and have their opponents staring down the barrel. The game winds on, and Banyana Banyana just cannot find a way through the stubborn Zambian defence. In the 72nd minute, Zambia scores yet another goal, and the South African players look to the skies for answers. A commentator quips: "Well that goal all but confirms what we have known the whole day, Zambia are in the final."

The stadium is in a state of ecstasy as they watch South Africa get put to the sword. Thembi is not ready to kneel just yet though. With 15 minutes to go, Banyana Banyana get a corner, the ball lifts over the keeper and sails to the far stick, a towering South African striker meeting the cross with her head to pull one goal back. Three minutes later, and Thembi is like a wild cat that refuses to be caught. She performs tricks rarely seen on the world's best stages, slicing through three defenders and leaving one lying on the ground. Thembi enters the box and steps over the ball once, promising magic to follow. The defender senses it too and swipes her leg out to Thembi's like a machete to branch. Thembi goes down, hurt, and South Africa are awarded a penalty. After the goal is converted by Leandra Smeda, the score is 3-2. In the 83rd minute, a Zambian nightmare begins to turn real at the sight of Thembi Kgatlana ripping down the left wing again. She dusts off two defenders and enters the box close to the out-line and cheekily sends the ball with the outside of her boot into the box; it gets slotted home by another player in green, Rhoda Mulaudzi. The stadium falls into echoing silence as the Zambians watch their team fumble a three-goal lead. The game goes to penalties, and South Africa win. Football has a habit of breaking hearts.

In the final, South Africa come up against the hosts, Zimbabwe. Thembi has flashbacks of the Olympics and being faced with a hostile and one-sided crowd. There is not a spare chair in the house.

Thembi scores the first goal right at the end of the first half. After the halftime break, Zimbabwe find inspiration from the home crowd and squeeze out an equaliser. Just as it seems Zimbabwe are finding their groove, Thembi comes up with an idea to switch positions with the striker. The change leads to a confusing passage of play, whereby a ball is swung in to meet the diving header of Leandra Smeda, who secures the 2-1 victory and the COSAFA Cup for Banyana Banyana. During the awards ceremony, Thembi is named Player of the Tournament.

Shortly after the tournament Thembi's phone rings with a familiar number, but one not seen in a long time.

"Hello, Vera."

"Hello, Thembi. Did you hear the news?"

"What news?"

"You're speaking to the new head coach of Houston Dash."

"Ah that's great, Vera. Congratulations!"

"Yes, it is. Now pack lightly. It's warm this time of year."

"Excuse me?"

"Don't make me spell it out, Thembi! How would you like to come join me in America?"

CHAPTER 23

What Is the Purpose of Your Visit to America?

Signing with an overseas football club means filling out forms, sourcing documents – and keeping secrets. Sometimes word getting out at the wrong time can ruin the deal. There is one person Thembi wants to tell that she has signed for Houston Dash more than anyone – Linda Motlhalo. They have been through everything together. From under-10 Gauteng football through the HPC all the way to university. In the off season, Thembi and Linda spend a lot of time together catching up at each other's places, or going for lunch or just for a walk. They are out for ice cream one day, and it is killing Thembi to not tell Linda. Keeping a secret from Linda is so unnatural that she fears it may just be showing on her face. Thembi looks at Linda. She looks disappointed. She can feel Thembi's secretive energy. The guilt is bubbling inside Thembi. She does not know how much longer she can keep Linda in the dark like this. Suddenly, Linda turns to Thembi, looks into her eyes and puts her hand on her shoulder.

"Thembi, I have something to tell you."

"Uh... Okay?"

"I'm not supposed to though. I could get in big trouble."

"Okay, what is it, Linda?"

"Thembi, I have signed for Houston Dash in America."

Thembi bursts out laughing. The whole restaurant turns and looks as the two girls jump up and embrace. Thembi puts her hands on Linda's shoulders, pushes her back slightly and looks in her eyes, wearing a smile of sincerity.

"Linda, I'll see you there."

When Thembi tells her parents the news, they are sceptical. Her mother stands in the kitchen, drying a plate, when Thembi informs her that Vera Pauw is going to be the coach of the team. Her mother stops wiping and stares at Thembi, through her eyes straight to her soul.

"Vera? Vera? The same Vera who only thought you were good enough to play 10 minutes for Banyana Banyana? What makes you think it will be so different now?"

Thembi cannot help but sneak a small smile. She remembers standing in this very kitchen as a child while her parents cursed the very idea of her playing football, and now they are passionate supporters, in the know about all the characters and elements of the game, with their own set of criticism for coaches and players. Thembi finds it joyously endearing.

Janine van Wyk is already signed to Houston Dash, so when Thembi and Linda join her, there will be a fierce trio of South African warriors on American shores.

BEFORE THAT CAN HAPPEN THOUGH, Banyana Banyana play in the 2018 Cyprus Women's Cup, a 12-team international tournament. Banyana Banyana limp their way through, labouring out average results and eventually finishing up in sixth place. After their last game, the players are tired and keen to make their way home. However, a tournament official pays them an unexpected visit. She tells them that they cannot leave just yet, one of the South African players has been nominated for an award and the team is requested to wait until the awards ceremony after the final. The players watch from the stands as Spain handles Italy in the final. After the trophy is lifted, a deep Cypriot voice booms over the speakers,

"And the Player of the Tournament is... Thembi Kgatlana from

What Is the Purpose of Your Visit to America?

South Africa."

Thembi is staring down at her phone when the announcement is made. She hears her name, looks up and around, squinting in confusion. It cannot be. Of the 12 nations in this tournament and the almost 300 players competing, they have chosen one small player from the sixth-placed nation as the player of the entire tournament? It is an achievement that speaks for itself.

Thembi is still in awe of the award she received when she wakes up the next morning. She has to put the celebrations aside for now though. She is still hacking through a forest of admin. She needs to arrange an American work permit before she can play for Houston Dash. She visits an embassy in Cyprus to try and resolve the matter but is bounced at the front door. She has no option but to board the USA-bound plane with Linda and Janine without a permit. The trio lands in Portland, Oregon. As they navigate the complex and unfamiliar web of American airport security systems, a gloved hand holds Thembi back.

"Excuse me, Ma'am."

"Ah, hello."

"Let me see your documents please."

Thembi fumbles in her bag and shoves the dark-green passport and some papers at the official.

"You're here for occupational reasons?"

"Yes, I'm here to play football, professionally."

The words sound good coming out of Thembi's mouth. She cannot help but let a smile ease across her face. That ease is shattered though when the official asks his next question: "Where is your work permit, Ma'am?"

"Ah, you see, the thing is..."

"Please step this way, Ma'am. Come with me."

The official is a serious man, with a serious suit and serious glasses, just like in the movies. He signals to another one of his kind, slightly taller but just as serious. The taller official touches an earpiece before approaching and helping guide Thembi to the side. Thembi, caught up in the cinema of the moment, does not get a chance to consult with Linda or Janine, or even grab her bags. She gets whisked swiftly away to a dimly lit room with a cold metal table as a centrepiece and a mirror for a window.

"Ma'am, what is your purpose for being in America?"

"I told you, I'm here to play soccer."

"Soccer? You're a soccer player? That's what you do? You play soccer?"

"Yeah, I've just signed for Houston Dash, I'm going to be playing in the upcoming…"

"Houston Dash, you say? You see, Miss *Kat-Lan-a,* there are already holes in your story. If you are supposed to be playing in Houston, then what are you doing in Portland?"

"Well, we have a pre-season game against the Portland Thorns."

"That's what they all say."

Thembi throws a puzzled look at the official.

"*Who* all says that?"

"I'll be asking the questions here, Ma'am. Where have you just come from?"

"We just finished a tournament in Cyprus and now…"

"Cyprus? Okay, Cyprus. What was the nature of your visit in Cyprus? Did you pick up anything new in Cyprus that we should know about?"

"Well, I guess, I picked up a Player of the Tournament award and brought it here."

The taller official leans in and whispers into his partner's ear. The shorter official listens for a few seconds before holding his hand up and demanding silence from his partner.

He keeps his eyes on Thembi while he reaches into his pocket and slides out his phone. He looks down at it, opens Google and quickly taps his thumbs on the screen. He tilts the phone to show his partner. They both look up at Thembi, down at the phone, and then look at each other and nod their heads.

"Congratulations on your award, Thembi. You're free to go."

Thembi stands up and shoots out of the door. She knows that there are not too many minutes between this moment and when their connecting flight takes off. Thembi does not bother to go back for her bags. She puts her faith in the kindness of her teammates and that they would have grabbed them for her. She makes the flight with 10 minutes to spare.

The team plays the pre-season tournament, and Thembi sets off on her next mission: to obtain her work permit. Thembi and the Houston Dash assistant coach Lisa Cole fly straight from Portland to Seattle. They pick up a rental car and drive through the night towards Vancouver, reaching the Canadian border at 1am. The authorities at the gate look at the two shivering women. They check their passports.

"You're from Africa, Ma'am?"

"Yes, from South Africa."

"Why are you trying to enter Canada?"

"I need to get an American work permit from Vancouver."

"Ma'am, as a South African citizen, you need a Canadian visa to cross this border."

Thembi and Coach Lisa turn the car around and begin the six-hour slog back. A defeated silence fills the car, as the realisation dawns that Thembi is going to have to go all the way back to South Africa to get her papers.

Thembi hops the several time zones between America and South Africa and feels nothing but anxiety on the flight back as she pictures her teammates training harder and gelling tighter in her absence. She spends a week at home visiting her parents and at the end of it she walks away with a work permit and the desire to get going.

When Thembi returns, she cuts a lonely figure in the Houston Dash training room. Janine and Linda have both been accepted into the new pack, they have inside jokes with the other players, they have socialised with them and they know their style of play much better than Thembi. She has to catch up on her own.

America feels like Mars. Houston is in the heart of Texas, where everything seems to be a bit bigger than normal. From the sky to the food and the cars, it is supersized America at its grandest. Thembi finds pockets of home within Texas. She shares their passion for beefsteak and chicken wings. But still, there's something in the meat that tastes far from home.

Thembi takes time to adjust to the level of professionalism at the club. Most of the players have trained professionally since they were 12 years old, and they play nationally for the best women's nations in the world – Australia, China, America and Argentina, just to name a few. They have all been groomed for this stage. Thembi has just been thrown into the ring and told to box. They are all much more accustomed to the everydayness of being a professional; the little things, like the early risings and proper nutrition, sports massages and ice baths – Thembi Kgatlana hates ice baths with a passion.

If you want to see me cry, put me in an ice bath.

Thembi's first Houston Dash game is against the Chicago Red Stars. It is the first time in Thembi Kgatlana's life that she has ever seen snow. It is the coldest she has ever felt in her life. The kind of coldness that originates from your bones and oozes outwards. Vera gives Thembi a clear set of instructions for the day: "I want you to forget the cold. I want you to forget America. I want you to forget whatever might be going on at home. Today, you must become a student of football. Find the player who will be playing against you, learn her every move, never take your eyes off her, and if I bring you onto the field today, be ready to show me what you have learnt."

Thembi listens to the teacher. She locks her eyes on the target: the Chicago left fullback. She watches the way she runs, the way she tracks backwards, the way she breathes and the way she ties her shoelaces. Thembi's feet begin to itch. She knows she is about to make this defender's life hell.

With the scores deadlocked at 0-0 in the 80th minute, Vera tells Thembi to warm up. It is a familiar sight and sound; Vera turning to Thembi with just 10 minutes to spare. Thembi unleashes onto the field like a bullet out the chamber. Her short sprints and tricky ball control add an electricity to the game that was previously missing. Before long, Thembi's opposite number is gasping for air, her hands are on her knees, she looks up at Thembi, wondering where on earth this woman came from and what possesses her to run like this. Thembi smiles and sets off on another run. She gets

What Is the Purpose of Your Visit to America?

behind the defender with ease, pushes the ball down the wing and then swings a sweet cross into the box. Her teammate finds the end of the pass and taps it in for Houston Dash to win the match 1-0.

Ten minutes. To most people, 10 minutes is 10 minutes. The time one might take to make a coffee, have a shower or read the news. For Thembi though, 10 minutes is all she has. Her livelihood, her dreams, every wall she has broken through to be at this point. It all hangs in the balance, resting on 10 precious minutes. It forces Thembi to go into this mental zone, one that helps stretch each of those minutes into a lifetime in her mind.

GAME AFTER GAME, THEMBI watches from the bench. Her feet tap and her legs shake; she is like a chained wild animal, itching to spring from this bench and go hunting. Vera rarely looks at her though; she only looks straight ahead. She focuses on the other players, giving instructions, compliments and criticism. With 10 minutes to go, inevitably, she will turn to Thembi: "Feel like helping us out there? Go get those legs warm, Thembi."

Opposing teams come to know that the last 10 minutes against Houston Dash are draining, as every time – guaranteed – that small woman from South Africa will enter the field and rain down terror on anyone standing between her and the goal.

The fans come to know and love Thembi. They are instantly attracted to her addictive smile and bouncy personality. When they see her on the field, they come to love her as both a player and a person. They too are very accustomed to Vera's tactics by now. As the season flows on, every time the clock strikes 80, the Houston Dash fans will instantly be on their feet, clapping, whistling, singing, and chanting: "It's Thembi time! It's Thembi time!" They turn to each other and hug, "It's Thembi time!"

True to form, Thembi will come on and give the fans the most enthralling 10 minutes one could witness on a football field. The price of the ticket justified through the skill of Thembi's boot.

I had to constantly be talking to myself. The thing is not to ask why this is happening but rather what you can do about it? If I only have 10 minutes, so be it. For those 10 minutes I will be the hardest player on the planet. They will be played like my last 10 minutes on earth. If 10 minutes is what I got, then 10 minutes is what it is. That's Thembi time.

Towards the end of the season, Thembi is once again brought on in the final minutes in a game against the Portland Thorns. By this stage, she is charged half with inspiration and half with frustration at the fact that she is still limited to just the final plays of the game. Against Portland Thorns she brings a different kind of fire, an aggressive, unrelenting style of football. Once the 10 minutes are over, and the players are exchanging shirts and hugs, the coach of the Portland Thorns takes Thembi by the arm and pulls her aside,

"What is your name?"

"Thembi Kgatlana."

"Where are you from?"

"South Africa."

"Okay Thembi Kgatlana from South Africa. I have to tell you that you are one of the most incredible players I have ever seen in my life. A word of advice – make consistency your goal."

The word sticks in Thembi's mind like a cloud hovering in front of the sun. A cloud that just won't go away. *Consistency*. She first has to define what the word means for her. She knows it is not something that she can just achieve in one go, or over two weeks or even a year. The one thing Thembi knows is that consistency means forever, and she intends to be great forever.

CHAPTER 24

Save the Brother

There is a lot on Thembi's mind as she settles into life in America. She is glad to have a piece of home with her: Janine and Linda. Janine definitely takes on the mother's role in the trio.

"Thembi just brightened every day for me," Janine recalls, "even though some days she disturbed my rest. Linda and Thembi would ask me to drive them to the shops, because they could not drive then."

They are certainly a long way from the streets of Randfontein. Thembi knows, as she walks down these American avenues, that she wears the pride of her family on her back, and no matter how far she may stray, home will always be in her – for better or for worse.

Thembi is out looking at new clothes with Linda one day when her phone rings. Linda stops browsing when she feels a coldness coming from her friend. She looks at Thembi, and she knows immediately that she is looking at a woman receiving bad news.

Tumelo is released from prison after serving six of his 15 years. This time, he emerges with something different in his step. His eyes are full, his chin is up, and his tongue is sharp. He tells anyone with an ear that he is a changed man, and that the community can feel safe about letting him back in. He moves back into 70 Mohapi Street. Thembi's uncle and mother are delighted to have him back. But her father remains silent and suspicious. Tumelo is undeniably better than the last time he was in this house though. He is engaging, asking everyone how their day was, offering to help carry groceries and clean dishes. He talks about the weather and going for walks, normal family things to talk about. When he leaves the house, he sings and whistles and greets passers-by as he slides down the road.

There are only so many roads in Mohlakeng, and some of them lead to dark places. There is a hostel in Mohlakeng, a well-known hostel. It is a tough place. Chipped paint. Broken windows. Burning tyres. Young men, drowning in drugs and violence. Tumelo sometimes passes by and greets those hanging out on the stoep. He knows some of them from before; others he knows from prison. There is one such character who is often seen hanging out in the corner of the stoep – John.

You will see John with his hat drawn over his eyes. The toothpick flicking up and down is a constant feature in the corner of his mouth. He is not particularly large, his jeans sag low, and his sleeveless vest shows off modest arms. Despite being physically unassuming, John is a much feared man in the community. John earns money by selling nyaope in the hostel. He does some of the work himself, but when there is enough business, he sometimes deputises someone else to deal for him. He prefers dealers who do not use nyaope themselves, for obvious reasons.

John sees Tumelo walking past one day, gives a sharp whistle and nods in Tumelo's direction. Tumelo walks over, not rushing, keeping his hands in his pocket.

"Say man, aren't you that guy that just got out of prison?"

"That's me."

"And you clean now?"

"Sparkling clean."

"Do you need money?"

"Who doesn't need money?"

"Alright. You sell the rest of this nyaope, this time, I'll give you 10 per cent, if you do a good job, next time I will give you 20 per cent. Keep it up, and you'll be a rich man. What do you say?"

"Cool, I can move it."

John hands Tumelo the nyaope. He turns and walks out of the hostel. He checks once over his shoulder before veering off left. He walks straight to a friend's house, knocks on the door and enters. They close the door, close the blinds, switch off the lights and they do not leave for the next three days. On the fourth day, John begins to wonder what has become of his investment. He begins to ask around town. People say that they have not seen Tumelo in days, but if they had to bet on it, all the nyaope is probably inside Tumelo and his friends. John begins to dig a little deeper and finds out where Tumelo lives.

IT IS A WARM SATURDAY EVENING. Thembi's mother, her uncle and her father all sit down for a family meal. Thembi's mother drops her fork as the shrill of screeching tyres fills their otherwise quiet street. A car door slams open and shut, and a vicious knock raps on the front door of the house. Thembi's uncle slowly puts his plate aside, pushes his chair back and heads for the door. He opens it slightly, looking at John through the crack.

"What do you want?"

"Where is Tumelo?"

"What do you want here?"

"Hey! I said, 'Where is Tumelo?'"

"He's not here."

"Then tell me where he is."

"I don't know where he is."

"Listen to me, old man. I will come back here and burn this house down. Don't play me."

Thembi's uncle kicks the door fully open and grabs John by the shirt. John throws the first punch, and before long, the two men are entangled on the floor, hammering each other with fists, while Thembi's father attempts to separate them. Her mother is crying. John throws two more vicious blows before climbing off of Thembi's uncle. Both men are hurt, bleeding like open taps. John stands, breathing heavily, points a finger at the rest of the family and promises to return before walking back to his car.

It takes many days for Thembi's uncle to recover and his wounds to heal. The conversations around the house are muffled, defeated. The dark side of Tumelo has returned. What makes it difficult to discipline Tumelo is that beneath his addiction, he has a heart. He does not mind apologising for his mess-ups. He honestly – and painfully – admits that he is human, made of mistakes, full of potential, and riddled with problems. Tumelo also loves Thembi. No matter how bad he gets, no matter what dark corner of whichever shebeen he may find himself in, he always finds time to talk about Thembi, his younger sister.

Thembi decides to try one more time. She sends money back home for Tumelo to go for rehabilitation treatment. Thembi calls Tumelo and calmly explains that this is for the best, that she loves him and she does not want to see his potential disappear and him go to waste, like so many other men in the community. He hesitantly agrees to go.

The first few days of rehab are rough. Sleepless nights, sweaty sheets, scratching arms and hearing things. But things get better. Through the group therapy and nature walks, the cigarette smoking and the midnight talks – things get better. Tumelo gets better. He helps out around the centre, tending to the gardens, talking to the other patients and making the orderlies laugh. He plays cards, teaches other patients new games and – as always – brags about his little sister.

One cold Thursday, around midnight, the orderlies are awoken by a noise, followed by a number of other noises – none of them sound good. They pull on robes and run down the hall. A sprinkling of blood leads them to the kitchen, where one patient is seen in the corner, gripping his stomach, blood streaming through his fingers. In the opposite corner of the room is Tumelo, breathing heavily, sweating steadily, and holding a knife in his right hand. He looks at the other patient and then diverts his gaze up to the orderlies standing at the entrance of the room, unsure of what to do next. Tumelo drops the knife, runs out of the door and back onto the streets.

The thing about addiction is, it convinces you to trust it. He could be so clean for a month, or however long it took for you to lower your guard. Then he hits you again. I realised that, these things out there on the street, he will always want those things more than he wants to be helped. There comes a point in an addict's life where only they can help themselves. Addiction is tough for everyone around it. Imagine me trying to become a superstar, and all I get on my phone from those closest to me is bad news. But, sometimes, when I had the strength, I used it as the fuel to power me. I demanded better for myself than that. I decided that I will not let myself be dragged down by the scars of my family. I have to look at myself as the one who has the opportunities that the rest of my family don't have.

CHAPTER 25

I Thought You Were Better

The season finishes in America. Thembi, with the 10 minutes she has been given here and there, manages to rack up two goals and three assists, decent statistics for an impact player. As Thembi walks around the grand streets of Houston, she has a feeling in her bones, something from within that tells her that greatness is on its way. Something that tells her to push on, no matter what forces try to hold her back.

The three South Africans playing for Houston Dash board a plane in early September 2018. The bonds between Linda, Janine and Thembi have grown stronger over their time in America. Their sisterhood pulled Thembi through dark, lonely and homesick moments. They could easily tell when she was feeling distant and defeated and would make sure to lift her spirit in their own unique ways. Thembi is grateful to them, and as they fly over the Atlantic Ocean, the three players know that they are returning to their national team as more complete footballers.

The women land in Johannesburg. They get a handful of hours to embrace their loved ones before boarding the next flight, to the Windy City – Port Elizabeth (later Gqeberha). When they arrive to join the team in camp, Coach Des pulls the three Houston Dash players aside.

"We understand the travel you've just done and the time zones you've just crossed," she says. "You girls must be shattered. You are all integral to the team, but we are going to rest you at the beginning of the tournament, just until you've recovered."

Thembi is relieved. The rest is needed, plus, she is hesitant to start this tournament. Thembi's name is said more often these days, in corridors, in barbershops, in opposition changerooms. People know that the missile from Mohlakeng has just won Player of the Tournament for two international competitions in a row, and completed a season for one of the biggest women's football teams in the world. The pressure sits heavy on her shoulders, impossible to ignore and difficult to move with. Thembi has a conversation with herself before the first game. In order to be consistent, like the Portland Thorns coach urged her to be, she needs to become less of an individual and more of a teammate. She decides that during this tournament she will pass instead of shoot, cooperate instead of compete, encourage instead of excel. For this tournament, Thembi plans to play egoless football.

There is something about this Banyana Banyana squad. They have achieved a number of things that other teams try, but often fail to do. They have kept the same faces around season after season. They have cried together, lifted gold together and grown together. There has only ever been one Bafana Bafana player to achieve more than 100 caps for the country. In Banyana Banyana, there are eight players with more than 100 caps for the nation. It also feels as if they are just getting started.

Banyana Banyana honour their home crowd in the best possible way. They dispatch all of their opponents, including a 6-0 slaughter of Malawi in which Linda Motlhalo scores a hattrick. South Africa go on to win the tournament, largely without Thembi's help.

Thembi feels as if she achieves her goal of playing more for her team than for glory, but she is not sure if it is worth it. All round she has a very average tournament, scoring no goals and receiving no accolades. After the tournament, a COSAFA official even feels it necessary to rub salt on her situation: "Thembi, I am so disappointed in you. I thought you were more of a complete footballer after the last tournament. But today, you looked like you had no energy out on that field. I guess I was wrong about you."

Thembi knows there is an element of truth to it, but that is overshadowed by her annoyance at the fact that opinions seem to flow most heavily when you are at your lowest.

Part of being a successful footballer – and human – is the ability to bury disappointment quickly and lift your chin soon after. For Thembi, this is not really a choice at this point in time. In the following three months, the AWCON will begin. This is not just any AWCON though: the top three teams of this year's tournament will gain automatic qualification to the World Cup, the most prestigious tournament any player can hope to attend. A tournament that no South African woman has ever attended. Next year's tournament is in France. Thembi's mind runs wild with thoughts of standing under the Eiffel Tower with her teammates, but there is a long battle required before that becomes a reality.

CHAPTER 26

What Do You Want from Paris?

When Thembi is busy preparing for the AWCON, she gets an email from Nike. They've seen her, they want her; Thembi Kgatlana needs a swoosh under her name. The company says it's getting serious about women's football. They want to kick off their programme with a celebration of Thembi. Nike announce a competition, calling out to artists across the world. The challenge is to create an artwork featuring Thembi Kgatlana. Artists from all over the globe pick up their paint brushes and answer the call.

There is one in particular that Thembi instantly feels love for. It is something truly unique. A Cape Town-based artist, Danielle Clough, has a really distinctive way of creating art. She uses the vintage technique of embroidery, which involves sewing and stitching colourful cotton threads together to form a picture. Her Thembi piece is breath-taking. Thembi appears in splashes of purple, blue, green, yellow and pink, staring over her left shoulder in a subtle salute to her past, but her shoulders face forward, giving the impression of a battle yet to be fought. She appears against a bold orange background. The artist says her medium is a metaphor for Thembi and all other women who have to weave their way through the obstacles that stand between them and a dignified life. Thembi sees the piece on Instagram and instantly falls in love with it. In a direct message, the artist reaches out to

Thembi and says that she is more than happy to gift the star with the artwork. Thembi swears from that day forward, that in any place she lives, that piece of art will be the first thing any guest who enters her house sees.

Banyana Banyana board a flight to Accra, Ghana for the AWCON. Thembi is like an excitable child on the flight over. She walks up and down the aisle, sending the same energy out into every row, "Guys, we are going to the World Cup this year."

Thembi walks up to her captain, Janine. She is sleeping, her cap covering her face and her earphones blocking out noise. Thembi shakes Janine awake.

"What is it, Thembi?"

"You know what, Janine?"

"What?"

"We are going to go to the World Cup."

The corner of Janine's mouth curls up into a smile as she turns over to go back to sleep. "Let's not get so ahead of ourselves, Thembi."

Thembi walks up to the next row and wakes up the next teammate.

The players set up camp in Ghana, and the intensity is there from the first training session. The players are fit and fired up, getting stuck into each other in healthy, heated competition. As the players walk off of the field from practice, Thembi runs up to Janine again, and talks right into her ear.

"Janine, we are going to the World Cup."

Janine sighs: she has been to many AWCONs and has had World Cup glory within grasp before, and they have only ever come up short. She is a custodian of disappointment.

"Thembi, we mustn't get too excited. I have seen this before. We give it a good fight, and we always fumble it."

Thembi hardly hears Janine. She just makes sure to remind her captain after every training session that they are going to France.

"Janine, what is the first thing you are going to buy in Paris?"

"Stop it, Thembi."

Just before the tournament, South Africa have a warm-up

friendly against the home nation, Ghana. It is a game South Africa is happy to play before – and not during – the tournament. The crowd, the field, the weather and the fortune all seem to be against South Africa. Ghana emerges victorious, 1-0, but Banyana Banyana definitely show some signs of resilient football.

In the changeroom after the game, as Thembi and Janine untie their boots next to one another, Thembi whispers into Janine's ear, "Janine, I've got a feeling, this is going to be our year."

"Thembi, I'll believe you when I am holding a ticket to Charles de Gaulle Airport."

The players return to their hotel. Thembi walks straight up to her room. She gets down on her knees and she prays. She has been praying a lot recently, thinking about those 10 minutes. Thinking about the small window of opportunity she has been given up until this point. She prays for more. She asks for the window to crack open just a little wider.

Ever since the draw for the AWCON groups, South Africans have been brutal on social media in their predictions of Banyana Banyana's chances. The common sentiment is that the South African women will be out of Ghana by the end of the group stages, watching the final on television at home. The first game is against Nigeria, nicknamed the Super Falcons – Banyana Banyana's playground bullies. In 2014, the last time South Africa had an opportunity to go to the World Cup, it was Nigeria that slammed them out of the tournament.

The game is scheduled to be at 6pm. If left to her own devices, Thembi can dream away many hours of the morning. On the day of the game, Thembi wakes up after a titanic 11-hour sleep. As soon as she forces her eyes open, she knows she is in trouble. She has overslept. She blinks hard, she tries to wipe the grogginess from her eyes but only massages them closed again. She can barely summon the strength to scratch her head. "Oh Jesus," she thinks to herself as she checks the time and sees the avalanche of messages from home wishing her luck for one of the biggest games of her life. Thembi drags her feet down the carpeted hotel stairs to the breakfast table. Her teammates tell her that she looks like a zombie.

Lifting her cereal spoon at breakfast feels like picking up a block of concrete. She speaks slowly, chews slowly and thinks slowly. Thembi excuses herself and pulls her lazy legs to the bathroom. She needs to find the fighter within her. *I was living but not alive.*

She splashes water on her face and thinks about the day ahead, about the game against Nigeria, about this first giant step to take in order to get to the World Cup. *The World Cup* – there is something about these words. They keep rolling around in her head, slowly settling into every corner of her mind. Thembi feels it coming, like the moment of silence before a flash flood comes rushing off of the mountain. She feels the nerves coming.

Before games, I get really, really nervous. I have to go to the bathroom a lot, but I know that is a good sign. I know if I am not feeling nervous, then something is not right. If the butterflies in my stomach go crazy, then I know my legs will too.

Thembi feels the energy return, she feels light on her toes and sharp in her mind. She feels it coming. She does not know what it is, but she can feel it in her bones.

When the team is announced, Thembi's heart sinks to her stomach. Her name is absent from the starting line-up. Her throat fills with doubt. She wonders what she has done wrong. How she could have trained – or prayed – harder. Her teammates even look to Thembi for reaction, but her face is stone cold. On game day, there is no time to entertain such thoughts. She has to bury them deep away in the backyard of her mind – and quickly.

I said to myself, "It's okay, Thembi. Not everything is about you. Be patient. Your time will come."

From the bench, Thembi does not restrain any passion. She yells at the top of her voice, encouraging her teammates, giving out tactical suggestions and cursing the referee. Around the 70-minute mark, Coach Des tells Thembi to warm up. Thembi jogs down the side-line; she does not take her eyes off the field. She stretches half-heartedly. She still does not take her eyes off of the field. She ends up behind the Nigerian goal, where Banyana Banyana have been putting in a decent effort to crack the Super Falcons' defence. Thembi stands behind the goal and is shouting so intensely for her teammates to score that she cannot hear her name being called. Eventually another substitute runs up to her and shakes her shoulder: "Thembi! They're calling you, you have to go on!"

It is the 80th minute. Of course it is. Thembi has 10 minutes to pull something off. Of course she does. From the side-line, Coach Des turns to give Thembi her instructions, but then they lock eyes, and she can see the world spinning. She knows that Thembi does not need instructions. She knows that the occasion speaks for itself.

"Just go out there and have fun, Thembi."

As Thembi is waiting for the all-clear to come on, the Nigerian coach notices her and begins to instruct her team: "Hey! Remember this one! Watch out for this one! She is the tricky one."

Thembi sprints onto the field, too excited at first, like a hungry tiger cub let loose in a chicken coop. Her muscles loosen, her spirit calms and she feels her focus sharpening. Around the 85th minute, Jermaine Seoposenwe chips a pass; it is the kind of pass that midfielders go to sleep dreaming of, immaculate in both line and length, the ball plonking down just behind the Nigerian defensive line.

Thembi Kgatlana is ripping down the wing. Two Nigerian players run up on each shoulder, trying to box Thembi in. The ball bounces in front of her. Thembi muscles through the defenders, takes three sharp steps and catches the ball on the volley. She puts her boot through the ball, sending it straight over the keeper's head and beautifully pinning it into the back of the net. Banyana Banyana erupt in raucous celebrations that have to be broken up by the officials. For the remaining few minutes, the Nigerian team focus their efforts on containing Thembi, but she is like a bee trapped in a moving car, impossible to catch and difficult to get near. This allows the minutes to grind down until the sweet sound of the referee's whistle signals the end of the match. Banyana Banyana are truly joyous; it is only the second time they have ever gotten the better of their West African rivals. Thembi Kgatlana wins Woman of the Match, despite only playing 10 minutes of the whole game.

Back in South Africa, many fans take to social media to

announce the pleasant surprise of waking up to the news that Banyana Banyana has beaten Nigeria. Not many knew that their national women's team was so badass.

The players have two days to prepare for the next game against Equatorial Guinea, another bogey team that South Africa just cannot ever seem to beat, another more physical African opponent that revels in the joy of outmuscling Banyana Banyana.

Thembi has not come down from the high of her hero moment against Nigeria. She is rewarded with a place in the starting line-up against Equatorial Guinea. She honours the opportunity with a sizzling performance. Thembi gifts three assists and slots home two goals as Banyana Banyana perform a 7-1 butcher's job on Equatorial Guinea. Thembi wins Woman of the Match for a second game in a row.

After these victories, the team does not explode in celebration. They walk off the field calm-faced, as if they have just finished another day in the office. Back home, Banyana Banyana is trending, with people suggesting that this team may just be the nation's best kept secret. Almost as if they have just been introduced to some of their own fans for the first time.

Thembi feels protective, as though the team now has something to defend, a lead that they simply cannot let slip through their fingers.

Next up: Zambia. Thembi bursts into the video analyst's room in the middle of the night.

"Give me the tapes!"

"What? Thembi, what's going on?"

"Give me the Zambian tapes. I need to see what I'm up against!"

She stays up late, watching clips. She puts in extra runs at practice, stays behind to practice extra shots – and prays more genuinely.

On game day, Thembi is bouncing off the soles of her feet and smiling. She smells blood. She laces up her boots and heads out the tunnel onto the field. The game begins with the intensity that is its due. Eight minutes into the game, the ball bounces outside of the box. The Zambian defenders stand back, knowing that the ball is too far from the goal to be scored. Thembi Kgatlana, anticipating the bounce, takes three quick steps towards the floating ball and connects a volley so crisp, the ball plays a note as it leaves her boot. The ball soars from metres away, picking up speed as it goes. The keeper has a better chance of catching a bullet and watches helplessly as it sinks from the top to the bottom of the rattling net.

Thembi's teammates run up to her. They rub and kiss her head as if she is the team's lucky charm. She is more than that of course – she *is* their luck.

Too caught up in the elation of Thembi's thunderous goal, Banyana Banyana lose focus and concede two minutes later. The game finishes in a draw. South Africa qualify for the next round at the top of their group. Thembi Kgatlana wins Woman of the Match for a third game in a row, the personification of consistency.

Now that the group stages are behind the team, there is something much heavier at hand. There is a daunting anticipation that haunts the air in the build-up to the semi-final against Mali. Thembi considers that this may be the biggest game of her life so far. If South Africa is victorious here today, they will qualify for their first ever World Cup.

Mali is a strong team, a continental bully on the football field, famous for breaking hearts at crucial stages of tournaments. The teammates find themselves saying less and less as they progress further in the tournament. There is less to be said, only more to be fought for.

Banyana Banyana start the game off cagey, still working some jitters out of their nerves. The first half feels longer than usual, the intensity stretching the seconds and minutes out like a piece of string. At around the 30th minute, Thembi finds herself inside the box when there is a fortunate moment, and the ball falls in front of her. She makes no mistake in pinning the ball to the back of the net and taking her nation one goal closer to the history books.

South Africa score another goal before the referee blows for the end of the match. The players drop to their knees in disbelief. Tears stream down their faces. Janine looks around in disbelief like a soldier on the battlefield once the fighting is done. She has fought, in this green and yellow jersey, for more than 100 matches, and never has she stood this high.

"So, Janine, what is the first thing you are going to buy in Paris?"

Janine turns around. Thembi is shooting her that familiar and cheeky smile.

Thembi embraces Janine. A tall blonde from Alberton and a short woman from Mohlakeng embrace. These two women were born in the same country but are from different worlds. And as they embrace in the middle of the field, unified and victorious, they both understand what a win like this means for the soul of their nation.

A country defined by its issues, plagued with challenges, but brimming with talent and thirsting for moments of pride – today Banyana Banyana have given them one of these precious moments. Social media explodes, celebrities and citizens alike pour their pride over Banyana Banyana's name like honey on a cake. One user jokes – "Minister of Sports, can we please organise an international friendly between Bafana Bafana and Banyana Banyana? We just want to see something…"

From the field, to the changeroom, to the bus, the team does not stop singing, "Amahlathi aphelile, akusekho ukucasha!" (There is no time to hide in the forest, it's time for war).

CHAPTER 27

A Starry Night in Senegal

In 2017, when Thembi lost out on the Confederation of African Football (CAF) African Women Footballer of the Year award, she accepted it. It hurt to hear another woman's name announced, but it was inevitable. She saw it coming. She was up against Asisat Oshoala, a dynamite striker from Nigeria. Asisat had won the award twice before, and she plays on the plush, professional grass of FC Barcelona Femení. Just to be invited to the award ceremony was honour enough for Thembi, but she quietly promised herself that next time she's in this room, it would not be for the event – it would be for the glory.

Thembi is home in Mohlakeng visiting her parents when she receives the news that she has been nominated for two 2018 CAF awards. She looks up from the email and sees her father sitting across the kitchen table from her, innocently sipping his tea. She takes a moment to appreciate the man before her. She thinks about how he has always pushed her to be better, how he has always fought to keep his family together. She thinks of his sacrifice, his pain, and how much of it is rooted in his love for her. She smiles at her father and asks him if he would like to accompany her to the CAF Awards ceremony in Senegal.

In the days leading up to the trip, Thembi helps her father to get a passport. As they climb the steps to the plane, Thembi's father looks nervous. He is flying for the first time. Thembi tells him to relax. They are flying business class, so a few hours of luxury and comfort await, way above the clouds. Thembi loves seeing her father in the plane. He's no longer scared. Instead, every corner of his face lights up with curiosity. Thembi laughs as she watches him navigate all the procedures that come with being a passenger on a plane: seatbelt, backrest, ordering food. When Thembi tells her father that he is about to meet some living legends, he does not believe a word she says. "It is cruel to tease an old man," he says. Thembi laughs again, pulls out her phone and takes pictures of her dad in the seat.

From the moment they arrive in Senegal, Thembi and her father are ushered along on a programme. They have two days before the ceremony, and the first stop is Gorée Island, off the coast of Dakar. CAF has organised for the players and some retired legends to visit a disadvantaged community on the island. Among the group, Thembi's father spots an unmistakable mop of black hair on a white neck – it is Bafana Bafana legend Mark Fish. Thembi's father can hardly control himself as he slides into the seat next to Mark and asks him about his glory days in the mid-1990s. Matlhomola's jaw almost hits the floor as he hears the news that he and Thembi are staying in the same hotel as some of these legends. He quietens down as his imagination runs freely. All the famous hands he might shake… Once they arrive at their destination, Thembi's father is just as enthusiastic to meet the community as he was to meet Mark Fish. He plays with the children, asks the elders questions and observes the community with empathy and respect.

Back at the hotel, Thembi is sleepy. She and her father each have their own room. Thembi feels somewhat responsible for his safety, given that it is his first time travelling out of South Africa.

"Dad, I'm tired. We have two hours to kill. Let's go chill in our rooms. I'm going to take a nap."

"What must I do?"

"There's lots you can do. You can watch TV, you can order food to your room – we can live like kings while we're here."

"Okay Thembi."

It's all marble, glass and mirrors in the lift up to their floor, and the hallway to their room is wrapped in a shiny maroon carpet.

"See you just now, Dad."

"I'll see you, Thembi."

Her father only pretends to put his key in the door while Thembi disappears into her room. Once she is in, he puts the keys back in his pocket, turns and heads back down the hallway to the lift.

The hotel lobby is buzzing with famous people and wheelie bags. Thembi's father first approaches the snacks table and samples three different kinds of "gently flavoured" water: cucumber, lemon and papaya. He builds a mound of food on a plate, scouts out a spot in the corner, pulls out a chair and takes a seat. He unfolds a newspaper and gently puts on his sunglasses, hiding behind them while he watches famous personalities walk in, players he had only ever seen on television or heard about on the radio as a child. In silence, he watches with fascination, whispering under his breath the name of every face he recognises. He keeps still, like a birder who has just come across a rare owl and wishes not to spook the moment away. When Thembi awakes from her nap two hours later, she knocks on her father's door and is confused when he does not answer. But she is overcome with joy when she comes down the stairs to the lobby and sees her dad talking to Lucas Radebe, giving the former Leeds star his personal analysis of the 1998/99 season.

The next day, CAF has organised a truly exciting event. Because the awards are in Senegal, the federation has invited the legendary Senegalese team of 2002 to take part in an exhibition game against a select group of legends from around the continent. The Senegalese team of 2002 famously made it to the World Cup quarter finals, only the second African team ever to reach this stage of the ultimate football tournament.

Thembi and her father take a seat in the VIP box to watch the game. Thembi recognises a few of the famous Senegalese players such as El Hadji Diouf, the former Liverpool sensation. Her father recognises them all. He tells Thembi about the goalkeeper and the stone-solid hands he has, he recalls statistics from seasons that passed decades ago. She is in awe of her father's encyclopaedic memory when it comes to football. He becomes emotional as he watches Samuel Eto'o dribbling with the same ferocity he had as a 21-year-old. As her father is pulled deeper into the game and narrating its characters, Thembi focuses more on him and less on the game. She is amazed at the facts in his head and how they attach to memories in his life, about where he was and what challenges he was facing when he was watching these giants in their prime.

Back at the hotel, Thembi's father wastes no time. He corners Samuel Eto'o and asks him a few questions about the Barcelona years. Thembi bids them goodnight and goes off to sleep. The next morning when she wakes, dresses and comes downstairs, her father is still in the hotel lobby, speaking to a different legend.

I don't know if he ever actually went back to his room.

It is 8 January 2019. The awards ceremony is scheduled to begin at 9pm. Thembi has the usual swirl of butterflies, but her nerves are eased by the calming presence of Coach Desiree Ellis. She too has been nominated for an award. Thembi considers for a moment the pain that will seep into her chest if she hears another woman's name being called out tonight. At just the thought of it, she can feel tiny cracks appearing in the corners of her heart. She breathes deeply and shakes her shoulders, letting the thought slide off and onto the floor; she has to keep a cool exterior for the sake of everyone watching her.

At the event, every detail has been considered, from the petals on the plates to the pictures on the wall, the event has that fragrance of glamour and success. Thembi is suited up and looking sharp. Her chin is up a little, out of pride.

Thembi's father is not allowed to sit next to her. The seat next to Thembi is occupied by Mohamed Salah and the one on the other side is taken by Sadio Mané.

As the evening's various hosts wade through the awards, Thembi blocks out the noise and thinks only about the big prize – Player of the Year. She faintly remembers that she has also been nominated for another award but at this moment cannot recall what it is.

Didier Drogba takes a few cool and measured steps while buttoning his blazer on his way to announce the next winner. He slides up the podium and turns to watch the big screen, which flips through an electrifying montage of the nominees for the African Goal of the Year. It can go to a woman or a man. Screens throughout the venue show videos of footballs rattling goal nets. Applause erupts after every clip. Didier Drogba purses his lips and nods his head slowly in silent approval. The last video clip shows Thembi Kgatlana masterfully looping the ball over the goalkeeper's head in South Africa's famous victory over Nigeria. Didier takes a moment – it looks like he's absorbing and appreciating the clip – before turning to face the audience.

He reaches into his blazer pocket and fishes out the envelope.

"And the award for the Goal of the Year goes to..."

He looks up and smiles, holding the crowd in comedically cruel suspense. Bit by bit, as if he were gently opening a fragile Christmas present, he tears open the envelope. As he reads the name on the card, he smiles and nods his head: "Chrestinah Thembi Kgatlana."

Thembi frowns in confusion. She looks up and around as if someone other than Didier Drogba had just called her name. She hardly recalls even being nominated for this award. She hesitates to her feet and makes off towards the stage. She wades her way through high-fives and applause, gracefully climbs the stairs and shakes Didier Drogba's hand before taking the trophy. The trademark Thembi smile is on her face, but it is not in full beam. Thembi does not want to process this award right now. She will celebrate it later. Winning Goal of the Year is a proud moment for Thembi, but it is just that – a moment. Scoring a world-class goal requires a few seconds of sound decision making, impeccable technique and good luck. But Thembi made a promise to herself, that she will be consistent in her every action. She planted the concept of consistency in her every action, from the way she ties her shoelaces to the way she eats. From the way she trains to the way she dreams. From her energy in the changeroom to her knack for demolishing opposition defenders on the field, leaving them in her wake, broken-ankled and broken-hearted as they watch her zigzag towards the goal. It is a familiar sight for many, seeing that Kgatlana 11 on the back of the shirt getting smaller as it pulls away from the rest of the pack. Tonight, Thembi's hunt for consistency will be marked. She will have passed if she can walk away as the Women Footballer of the Year – that is the boldest confirmation of consistency.

Thembi slowly walks back to her seat. She is surprised at how heavy the trophy is, but does not want it to show. She waves in joyous appreciation and then sits down in front of her father. He puts a reassuring hand on her shoulder. Although proud, he too is reserved. He knows his daughter, perhaps better than anyone else. He has never celebrated any hints of mediocrity in her life. Since she could walk, he has always pushed her to expect more from herself. There were times in Thembi's life when her father's motivation felt like cold cruelty, but as she feels his hand on her shoulder, she understands more than ever – he pushed her so that she could become greater than what society expects her to be.

The lights dim and the music plays again as the hosts prepare to announce the Footballer of the Year. Thembi closes her eyes, bows her head and prays. The monitors show videos of each of the nominees. Before Thembi, a familiar name flashes across the screen – Asisat Oshoala. The Nigerian sniper probably expects to walk away with this award like she expects the sun to rise tomorrow. The rest of the world expects it too – Thembi included. Still, she hopes. Thembi thinks back on her life. She thinks about the sacrifices made for consistency: the late nights, early mornings and long travels. Thembi also thinks about the place she is from, about the place of a young Black South African woman in the world, and what support she and her peers are given to achieve their dreams. She thinks about how she is from a country that has the wealthiest men's football league on the continent, but no professional women's league at all. Thembi feels herself sliding into a temporary pit of disappointment. Watching Asisat a few seats down from her, she wonders how a girl from Mohlakeng is ever supposed to compete with the world's best. She begins to negotiate with herself, telling herself that it might not be so bad should she miss out on the accolade two years in a row, but deep down she knows that it would be devastating. She hears a muffled voice in the background, but she is too focused on her prayers to clearly make it out. Two hands on her shoulders shake her out of her trance. Thembi cracks her eyes open and looks around – it is Coach Des who is shaking her, screaming into her ear, "Thembi! Thembi! It's you! They're calling your name!"

Thembi cannot move. Her expression is that of a young girl on her first day of school, frightened and overwhelmed. The piercing whistle bouncing off the ceiling is Thembi's father. He is overjoyed. He is standing on his chair, stomping his feet, whistling through his teeth and waving his hat around in the air. Just like he did when he saw his daughter score her first goal all those years ago.

Thembi is on her feet, but she is shaking. She feels weak, almost as if she has just stepped out of an ice bath. She takes her first step towards the stage. The clapping is deafening, sending Thembi into a kind of trance; she no longer sees the audience. As she takes her second step towards the stage, a movie begins to play in her mind. The walk is only about 10 seconds long, but it feels as if it is a two-hour feature film. Thembi sees the opening scene, fading in from black the dusty streets of Mohlakeng. The naughty childhood days. She remembers being teased for using the girls' bathroom. She sees little Thembi frightened in the corner – if only she knew whom she would become. She sees her brother Tumelo, drowning in his addiction. The movie plays on. She remembers America, Brazil, Cyprus and Zimbabwe, every unique corner of the world that she has been blessed enough to place her talented feet on. She thinks about all football has given her. Thembi thinks about the girl child in South African society, and she realises what is possible if she is just protected by those around them. Thembi allows the whole movie to play to the end, through the comedy, the drama, the suspense and the triumph, and then she looks up at the big screen above the stage and sees the words as clearly as stars in the night sky: 2018 African Women Footballer of the Year – Thembi Kgatlana.

Thembi stands at the stage, swallows the emotion and looks up into the bright lights. There are several generous rounds of applause before it all settles down – except for one man in the audience. Thembi's father stands tall, pride bouncing off his chin onto his chest and out into the world. He whistles louder, dances wilder and stomps his feet harder than he ever has before. His daughter is the champion of Africa, and the celebrations that spurt from his body in this moment are the embodiment of unconditional love.

The smile on my father's face after the announcement was the greatest trophy I will ever receive in my life.

Once Matlhomola Kgatlana's exhilaration has calmed down a bit, it is time for Thembi to speak. She opens her mouth and finds silence at the door. Thembi cannot help but chuckle at herself; she knows something that nobody else in this entire venue knows. When Thembi lost out on this award the previous year, she began writing her acceptance speech. When her teammates were in bed, she would stay up late in her hotel room, speaking into mirrors, jotting down notes in the mist on the shower glass and thinking up one-liners over room service.

Deep down, something told me to be prepared. I would say all these crazy things about women's football and how we need to change the system. I would laugh at myself, at some of the things I said. But whatever I had planned before, when I was standing up there holding on to that podium, nothing could come out. Absolutely not one thought I had over the previous year came to me.

Thembi lets some autopilot words of gratitude spill out of her mouth, and as soon as she lifts the award, she forgets everything she has just said. Once again, she is surprised at how heavy the award is. But she holds it close, pressing her heart to the trophy, introducing the gold to Thembi Kgatlana.

After the ceremony, Thembi is swamped with praise and salute. Some of the footballing world's biggest names, from Sadio Mané to Pierre-Emerick Aubameyang, reach their hand out to Thembi and extend their respect. They congratulate her on her goal, and tell her to continue on the path of greatness. Among all the adoration, someone pulls her away for a photograph with all the evening's other winners. When Thembi sees the photo a few weeks later, she jokes that its most defining feature is that she is the shortest person there. An old friends point out, "Thembi, you may be the shortest person in this photograph, but if you look carefully you will see that you are also the only person holding two trophies."

Thembi's father feels it his fatherly duty to inform the world that his daughter is a living legend. Waiting to travel home at the airport in Senegal, he reaches out to all and any passers-by to tell them the news. However, he soon realises that his efforts are actually unnecessary. All the strangers in this airport already know who Thembi is, how could they not? She is on every television screen, and her posts are being shared and retweeted all the time. Security guards, waiters and pilots abandon their posts at the sight of Thembi, and they rush to catch her for a quick selfie with the champion.

Back at OR Tambo International, Thembi believes the celebrations have died down. She is tired, on a steep comedown from the euphoria of the last few days. Thembi and her father barely talk on the long walk from the carousel to the arrivals gate. There is little to say. They have been consumed by praise and adoration for the past 24 hours, and their energy is spent. They have nothing to declare, and they exit the international arrivals door to the outside world, with Thembi still looking down at her trolly. An orchestra of applause, whistling and a thousand vuvuzelas fills up the airport's massive arrival hall. Thembi startles, panicked surprise masking her face. She looks around to make sure the applause is for her and nobody else.

Thembi switches on her smile and lifts a trophy high above her head. When she looks closer at the crowd though, she has an overwhelming sense of familiarity. She recognises these faces. She sees Mpho, her brother. She sees the reverend from her church and the old headmaster from her school. She sees her mother. Tumelo is there too. She sees the girls who used to tease her at school and the boys whom she used to leave in her dust on the athletics track. Each face triggers its own childhood memory. It slowly dawns on her that the whole of Mohlakeng is here. Buses were organised for the entire community, and members were escorted to the airport by the police. Thembi is speechless at the thought of it, all of these people who could have done anything else with their day, decided not to, just so that they could come out to celebrate their champion.

I really thought it was just going to be my family there, but I looked around at this whole community, some who decided not to go to work that day, others who had plans but cancelled them.

I realised that they were my family too.

Thembi embraces the people, wipes her tears and shares her trophy with the people who shaped her into the person she is today. Soon though, she must bid them farewell again. Thembi is due to join the Banyana Banyana camp in Cape Town for two serious internationals against tough Sweden and even tougher Netherlands.

Thembi and Coach Desiree sleep on the two-hour flight to Cape Town, both exhausted after another chaotic round of congratulatory commotion. (Desiree Ellis won the CAF African Women's Coach of the Year.) They emerge through the glass doors at Cape Town International, and once again they are ambushed by a wave of applause. This time, it is smaller but more personal. They look up to see the rest of the Banyana Banyana team. The players decided that it would only be fitting to give a hero's welcome to Thembi and Coach Des. They soften in the familiar embraces of their teammates. It is clear to Thembi that nothing but pride is exuding from her fellow players. This army has been through many battles together, they have faced nasty odds before but have bravely held on and emerged stronger from each fight. They have seen Thembi grow in ferocity and talent. They love that the little soldier has been awarded the medal of honour – and they make sure she feels the love.

CHAPTER 28

Homecoming

Most people change significantly after being announced as the best on the continent at their trade. For Thembi, the only thing that changes is the intensity of the fire that lights her passion. She tells herself that everything she is involved in on or off the pitch will be given that little bit extra. Anything in front of Thembi will be confronted with maximum effort and enthusiasm. Whether it is a press conference or a visit to an impoverished school, Thembi is going to leave a mark. She is going to be Thembi for the people.

Now, every time Thembi walks along the corridor or enters a corner store, she is greeted with: "Hey Kgatlana! From the TV! How are you?"

In the lead-up to two dynamite fixtures against the Netherlands and Sweden in January 2019, the team interacts a lot with the public, is active on social media and present at live activations. The city responds well. Something has always been bubbling in the air above Cape Town, something that brings out an enthusiasm for the national women's team. The games also feel like a homecoming celebration for Thembi and the team, a test against the world's best for this Banyana Banyana team, which has made its country sit up and take notice. The tickets sell out in three days.

It is a historic occasion, something that women's football in this country has never seen before, a packed-out home stadium.

But this is no ordinary Banyana Banyana team. This squad has proven that it can go toe to toe with the world's best. South Africa give a good, competitive account of themselves in the series. In the first game against Netherlands, the national team loses 2-1. Thembi Kgatlana scores the solitary goal. The second game sees both teams locked into a tense but goalless draw.

After the game, the players are permitted to make their way home. For Thembi, this means another set of festivities is looming. Her family has not seen her since she was named the African Women Footballer of the Year. They got to see her briefly at the airport, but they had to share her with thousands of fans then. Now they'll have their girl all to themselves.

Thembi's father wakes up early to buy meat and coal, and her mother prepares the pap. The last time a feast like this was prepared was when Thembi got her matric results. A lot of Thembi's peers who watched her grow are at the house, and join in on the celebrations. They truly understand the need to celebrate people who come from this community and go on to achieve success. Mohlakeng has produced boxing stars, musicians, athletes and many other great people, but this is a unique moment to celebrate one of their women heroes.

If I said I thought this would be possible growing up, I would be lying. You would have to be crazy to dream of making it as a woman footballer coming where I come from, where the only opportunities are for boys. Any hero who came out of here before is a man. I got the feeling that the community really needed it – a woman to look up to.

Especially the young girls from Mohlakeng follow Thembi around when she walks to the shops or goes to watch a local Sunday game. She can overhear them saying, "Yoh and she is so young, if Thembi can do it, then surely…"

When she goes for her morning jog, an army of children join her, laughing, out of breath, sprinting just to keep up with the champion. People stop their morning conversations on street corners and they stare.

"Hey, there goes that Kgatlana girl."

Even Tumelo has sobered up enough to celebrate his sister. He uses her name as a conversation starter, telling any ear that cares to listen about how his own flesh and blood is a superstar. For the first time, he is not known as Tumelo, the terror of the community. He is Tumelo, Thembi's brother.

Thembi's mother is fairly humble about her achievements. When people in her church group find out that her daughter is a Banyana Banyana star, they can hardly believe it.

"But why you never told us?"

Thembi's mother shrugs her shoulders in casual acceptance. She fully expected her daughter to be a star. Thembi's father is a quiet man on any day of the week that does not begin with an "F" or an "S", but when he goes out on the weekend, and the crispy froth of the beer meets his lips, he finds his voice. He shows his friends YouTube clips of his daughter raining down terror and chaos upon opposition defences and newspaper articles of her lifting trophies high above her head. Thembi's father is about the same height as her, so it is common for Thembi to give all her old jerseys away to him. He makes sure to wear a different one every weekend. His friends have become used to him kicking off every Saturday by walking up to them, clutching his shirt and then dramatically re-enacting the goal his daughter scored while wearing it. He speaks of how the lessons he taught her growing up instilled the champion mentality seen in her today. He is not wrong either.

Sometimes, though, Thembi just wants an ice cream. To just stroll to the shop wearing earphones and speaking only with her own thoughts. So she puts a bucket hat on and pulls it down low over her eyes. Most of the time it works. And even when her cover is blown, she still gladly takes a selfie with anyone and will always wear her million dollar Thembi smile.

When the Kgatlanas go out for a meal, the waiting staff often drop the bill in front of one of Thembi's parents, assuming that, as the elders at the table, they would be paying. Thembi always chuckles as she pulls the cheque towards her and reminds the waiter that she is in fact a dollar-earning overseas superstar – she will be the one to settle.

CHAPTER 29
Royalty

After two weeks at home, Thembi feels sufficiently celebrated, rejuvenated and grounded. It is time to hit the road again. Banyana Banyana have a date with the 2019 Cyprus Women's Cup, which announced Thembi as Player of the Tournament the previous year. Naturally, the expectations circling her name are cruising at a high altitude.

In the first game, to Thembi's surprise, she is starting on the bench. After 45 minutes, Banyana Banyana find themselves two goals down to Finland. At halftime, the coaches recognises that they need a firelighter. Thembi Kgatlana is brought on. She assists one goal and scores another to salvage a 2-2 draw for the national team. In the second game, Thembi is in the starting line-up against North Korea, but a horror show proceeds as South Africa get drilled 4-1. In the third game against the Czech Republic, Banyana Banyana seem to find somewhat of a groove and edge themselves one goal ahead in the first few minutes of the game. However, at halftime, some heavy and dark clouds loom on the horizon. An intense, flooding storm follows. Puddles gather on the field, and the women from South Africa find themselves struggling to play with the marshy conditions under foot. The cold-faced Europeans thrive in the moody weather conditions though, and by the time the final whistle is blown, Banyana Banyana are on the losing side of a 2-1 result. Thembi is left on the bench for that game too and the one after it. She feels the familiar hurt that comes with being excluded.

I mean, I could have been given a chance? Given my recent results.

Thembi spends days walking in circles, sulking at the ground. Whenever she gets to a place where she feels sorry for herself though, something stops her. A voice in the back of her head. Maybe it is her father's, maybe it is Sanele's from university. Maybe it is all these mentors she has had along the way who have always reminded Thembi never to allow her own drama to consume her.

I always arrive back in this same place – this thought, where I tell myself that not everything is about me. When these things happen, it is just life. Even if you become the best in the world, still, everything will not be about you. It helps to put yourself in other people's shoes. The players who got a chance to play in this tournament feel like this on every other day, when they are excluded and you are playing. Stay humble and patient.

After the Cyprus Cup, Nike invites Janine and Thembi to Paris, where the brand is launching jerseys for the upcoming World Cup with different sports superstars from around the globe. Thembi had seen a similar event on television four years ago. The likes of Cristiano Ronaldo and Sam Kerr in the finest tuxedos, posing for photographs with big flashes, a red carpet beneath their soles. At the time, Thembi told herself that she would feel that red carpet one day.

There is not a moment where Thembi and Janine are not treated like royalty. Usually, a dodgy handwritten sign awaits them at the airport, but today their names shine in golden letters. A warm-faced man in a suit walks up to them, grabs their bags, and starts to carry them without question. Usually, women footballers carry their own bags. They follow the bag-carrying suit-man outside and are guided to a sparkly Mercedes Benz C-Class. The man in the suit opens the door and motions for Thembi and Janine to get inside. They look at each other, mouths wide open in comic disbelief – women footballers usually take the bus. Thembi slides in and runs her hand over the leather seats as if they were made of gold.

Thembi has barely finished fiddling with the buttons on the roof when the car stops again. The driver informs the two stars that they have arrived at their hotel. Thembi goes to open the door but is beaten to it by the sharp-eyed doorman standing in front of the hotel's revolving golden doors. It is not often that Thembi finds herself speechless, but she has never seen a hotel like this. In fact, she has never quite seen a building like this. She did not know that human taste reached this level of opulence, and she cannot wait to see what it feels like to indulge in it.

Nothing is manual in the hotel, everything is automatic. One click of your thumb, and the scenery changes completely. The curtains are automatic, the tap is automatic. There is a television in the bathroom and a heated towel rail. The Champagne is from France, the cotton from Egypt and complimentary peanuts from Brazil. No detail has been spared, and Thembi notices every last one of them.

It is at this stage that Thembi's social media presence begins blowing up. She is gaining thousands of followers a day, and she is sharing the inner intricacies of the high life with them. Not for the purposes of showing off, but rather to show what you stand to get rewarded with if you put in the necessary grind and sacrifice.

The event is more than just a launch – it is a celebration of women athletes, and many different sports are represented. Thembi thinks there must be a mistake when she sees a small girl at a registration table. She considers asking if the little girl is lost, even though she doesn't look that way. Luckily, another athlete identifies her as Sky Brown, the youngest Nike athlete at the event, and a global skateboarding phenomenon. Thembi sees another figure walk in. She knows her just by her stance. There is something South African in her structure, something about the way she carries herself. Something in her body language says that she fully expects the world to be against her – and she is ready for the challenge. The athlete lifts her flat cap and looks around the room. Thembi meets her gaze and smiles. Caster Semenya smiles back before dipping her flat cap back down and disappearing into the crowd.

Royalty

Caster, Janine and Thembi take turns having breakfast and dinner in each other's hotel rooms. They laugh about the crazy ways of Europeans and frown at all the issues facing women back home, about the pandemic of abuse that currently plagues their land. They hardly have time to contemplate these things though. Nike has them on a busy schedule. Thembi thinks that the brand must know her better than she thought as no matter where they go, Thembi always seems to be within arm's reach of a snack.

That was my favourite part. I can be busy, but only if I have food in me.

The athletes even have to rehearse for the events.

Each athlete is assigned her own personal makeup artist. Thembi gets ready in a room that has her name printed on the door. She smiles into the mirror surrounded by light bulbs as the blush is brushed over her. For the first time, Thembi feels like the stars she used to watch on television growing up.

The athletes line up to take to the stage for the main event. Thembi brushes over her suit, loving the feel of the soft silk lapel. Suddenly, a small hand reaches up and grabs hers. Thembi gets a momentary fright. She looks down and sees a little girl, just a handful of years old. She looks down and sees little eyes, squinting to see her all the way up there, and a little hand reaching up, asking for guidance. Thembi looks down and sees the hope on the little girl's face, her excitement for life, her need for a role model and her desire to crush the task in front of her. Thembi looks down and sees herself.

CHAPTER 30

Dogs in the East

The biggest, wealthiest and best-run women's football league in the world can be found in China. But growing up, Thembi was sure that she wanted nothing to do with it. The concept of China used to scare the life out of Thembi. *Growing up, they used to tell us all these crazy stories about how people eat dogs over there. I remember listening to that and telling myself that I will never go live there, no matter what.*

However, one day Thembi's agent calls her and tells her about a team she has never heard of before – Beijing BG Phoenix. As Thembi considers the offer, she begins to think that maybe she was a little hasty in her judgement of the dog cuisine.

Transfer rumours, like bubbles, rise to the surface naturally. These rumours quickly make their way over the Atlantic Ocean to Houston Dash in America. Upon hearing that Thembi is even in negotiations with another club, Houston releases her from her American contract.

It is important to remember that in South Africa there is little to no provision for professional women athletes to make a proper living from their sport. The first time Thembi made a liveable wage was when she signed for Houston Dash. On the Beijing BG Phoenix contract, Thembi would be earning six times more than what she did in America.

Thembi flicks the lid off the pen and signs on the dotted line, and when people ask her whether it was all about the money, her answer is, *of course it was.*

Now there is only one thing left to do, and Thembi fears it will be very difficult. She needs to break the news to Linda Motlhalo. It feels as if she is going to inform her of the death of a loved one. Thembi hates to be the bearer of hard news. She and Linda have been friends since they were children. They were in the HPC together, they studied together, they played for the national team together and recently got lost and found their feet in America together. Thembi feels as though she cannot recall a time in her life when Linda and she were apart. The two friends meet up for lunch. Thembi is clearly distracted.

"Linda, I've got something to tell you."

"Okay..."

"It is going to be very difficult though."

"Okay?"

"I will not be flying back to America with you to join you for the next season."

Linda stops eating and stares at Thembi.

"I've got an offer, and I know it may seem rash, but I have to take it."

Linda puts down her fork, crosses her arms and lifts her eyebrows, indicating that she expects Thembi to explain herself further.

"It's just that it's the kind of opportunity that will only come to me once."

"Where?"

Thembi is startled by Linda's brash and loaded question.

"It's in, uh, China. There is this club called Beijing Phoenix."

Linda pushes her chair back, places her serviette on the table and coldly informs Thembi that she is going to the bathroom. Thembi's head dips into her hands. She feels her friend's disappointment and lets the guilt wash over her.

Linda's back. She slides a hand over Thembi's shoulder and says, "Thembi, I will see you in Beijing." She smiles.

THEMBI EXPECTS CHINA TO BE a world away, but when she gets there in January 2019, she realises that she is, in fact, in another universe. A six-hour time difference with South Africa makes it difficult to communicate with loved ones. Linda and Thembi are housed in a flat about five minutes away from the club. They are the only foreigners in the club. The rest of the team, all Chinese nationals, stay in a complex inside the stadium grounds. The grounds are a football factory, producing carbon copy players by the team load. Everything happens in the stadium. The players eat breakfast, lunch and dinner in the stadium. They study football in the classrooms inside the stadium. They enjoy their breaks in the stadium and they receive medical care in the stadium. Beijing Phoenix operates according to a strict schedule, one that Thembi and Linda struggle to adhere to.

They have breakfast at 7am. Have you ever heard of such a thing? No, we are still sleeping at this time.

The two South Africans have their own breakfast, and join the team in time for training. It is only a seven-minute walk to get to the fields. Thembi and Linda stay close on the walk, laughing and pointing at all the millions of things popping off on the street, and how different they are to anything seen on the streets back home.

The first training session at a new club is a little like your first day at a new school. There is always an air of awkwardness that hovers. The two South Africans stare at their Chinese teammates, who return the stare. They're ultimately suspicious of one another. The coach blows the whistle, and the warm-up begins. As Thembi and Linda watch the Chinese players go through their robotic stretches and slow jogs, they take a moment to have a quiet laugh between one another. It is clear they have been brought to Beijing to add some flavour and flair to the soup.

Although there is a lot of money in the Chinese league, the coaches still lack professionalism. Often Thembi finds herself talking to a coach on the training field through a cloud of smoke as they openly puff cigarettes during practice. Even the team doctors smoke. The Chinese players are disciplined though. They are focused, and they are tactically sharp. One thing they are not, however, is speedy. In the first training session, Thembi blitzes her teammates for two hours before the coach calls the session to an end. The rest of the Beijing Phoenix team stare in awe at Thembi and Linda. Many of them approach the duo, expressing delight at finally having some fire power in the squad. A few players keep their distance, sulking in the background; Thembi and Linda's presence could mean a place on the bench for them.

The year Thembi arrives in China, the league is cancelled to clear some space. It's a World Cup year and the congested calendar needs to be cleared some. Instead, there's a national Chinese tournament, involving teams from every distant corner of the gigantic country. Distances are lengthy in China, travelling is heavy, lugging bags between planes, buses and trains.

Most players sleep through the travel, able to doze off on demand. Thembi is a capable sleeper at the best of times, but in China she does not want to close her eyes. She does not want to deny her eyes the privilege of gazing upon something so fascinating. As one moves through China, everything changes. Different colours bleed into and out of one another. Depending on where the train stops, the shape of buildings change. The people dress differently, and they stare differently. They listen to different music, and treat animals differently. They cook noodles differently, depending on where the train stops.

Food is one aspect of Chinese life that fully has Thembi in a spin of curiosity.

In South Africa you can eat pap. *You can go to Limpopo, you will find it there. You can go to KwaZulu-Natal. You will find it there too. In China, if you are in the north or in the south, in the east or in the west, no two bowls of noodles are cooked the same.*

In Thembi's third game in China, a clumsy defender grows exhausted from chasing the South African fruitlessly around the field all day and puts in a jackhammer-tackle on her. Thembi hears the cogs in her ankle shift and snap. She hits the deck, grabs her leg and buries her face in the grass.

Frustration wells up in Thembi's mind every time she thinks about it. About how fragile this opportunity is, the one given to professional athletes. Thembi knows that every time her studs hit the grass, she is rolling the dice, risking her livelihood. She is one hot-headed tackle away from not being able to provide for her family. Some may say it is part of the skill of a footballer, to dance around such danger, but a defender intent on chaos is difficult to dodge. Thembi knows she has to care for her body; her two feet and the bones that support them are the tools of her trade. After all, she is not made of concrete. But Thembi sits alone at night, reflecting on how far she has come to get to this opportunity – and she realises that she is not made of glass either.

CHAPTER 31

Dutch Doctors

A specialist physio is flown in from the Netherlands. He is massive, blond and kind. He really struggles to enter the tiny Chinese doorways. His Dutch height may be incompatible with Chinese infrastructure, but the one thing he does have going for him is that he can strap an ankle better than anyone that side of the Euro-Asian border. He is kind to Thembi. He takes time to show her how to strap the ankle, carefully going over the movements and the flow of the tape. He even develops a little rhyme to help Thembi remember.

Thembi has time off, for observation, to truly take in this strange land under her feet and how the people in it live their life.

It's crazy, I thought it was so odd at first, how these people live. It is like they are all... one. You know, they don't see or do anything in China that the government does not want them to. In South Africa, we know about everything. The corruption, the crime, the scandal – we know it all. It stresses everyone out. There is a part of me that feels like it is always better to know than not to know. But I look at the people of China, and it's almost like they can just focus on their lives and enjoy themselves while the government takes care of the serious stuff. I'm sure there are a lot of things that the Chinese government is dealing with right now, but the people seem to know nothing of it. They don't need to, it is not their stress to bear. Walking in China, oh man you could walk in China, it is safe there. Sometimes, Linda and I couldn't sleep, and we would just go for a walk at midnight, down some moonlit street. It may be sad, but it's true that a South African woman does not leave her house without considering the possibility of getting raped and robbed. China was something different. I remember one day walking past this stream. It was a beautiful day. There was an old lady. She was just standing by the river, watching the leaves fall down onto the water. It looked like she had nowhere to be and nothing to worry about. Her face was calm, serene. She was just smelling the air, absorbing life, listening to the wind. That is a kind of peace we have not yet known in South Africa.

The training schedule in China is comprehensive. Players run their way through two hours of fitness in the morning and then another two hours' pure football in the afternoon. The hours in between are filled with video sessions, tactical analysis, physio torture or lifting metal. The strictness of the schedule and the strength of the strapping helps Thembi's ankle recover fairly quickly. The Chinese fans have already become familiar with Linda Motlhalo, the Randfontein Ronaldinho, but they have yet to meet Thembi Kgatlana.

One game in early 2019 changes this.

Thembi is technically still recovering, so she is kept on the bench for the first half. She suppresses a yawn as she watches her team crawl through a dreary first 45 minutes in which no goals are scored. Thembi is firing to come on to the field, but is met with frustration when the coach delays. She is not sure what the coach is waiting for, but when there are five minutes left on the clock, he gives Thembi a casual signal to go and play. Five minutes. There it is again. Thembi could scream out of frustration, but she channels her energy onto the field instead.

The mostly Chinese fans, who had all wandered off into the cyber abyss of their phones to escape the boringness of the game, suddenly take notice. Thembi is like a wild cat, darting to all corners of the field, stretching out the minutes, as if she only has five left to live. The fans swap to their camera apps and they record the missile from Mohlakeng. The ball goes out and the opposition defenders delay the throw-in, huddling instead, pointing at Thembi and devising a strategy. They talk through heavy breaths and heaving chests; they are visibly exhausted – and Thembi is just warming up.

And trust me, if you're playing against me, you don't want me warmed up.

While the players are busy finishing off their plan and the referee glances at his watch, Thembi steps off the field to grab a sip of water. As she returns, she notices an odd amount of space around her. In their paranoia, the Chinese defenders have forgotten to assign someone to actually mark Thembi. The ball comes to the Beijing left fullback, she boots a Hail Mary pass up the field, it sails directly to the head of the centre forward who pips it over to an empty space on the right wing that Thembi is hurtling towards, at belief-defying pace.

Linda is running just behind Thembi. These two women truly trust every word the other says. The ball bounces in front of Thembi, and Linda screams out to her, "Thembi, you have time!"

Thembi is far out from the goal, way outside the box. She hears every word Linda says, she even pictures her face as she is saying it, and then she thinks to herself: "Damn you Linda, I don't have time. Now is the only time."

The ball hangs in the air like a defenceless piñata. Thembi sees the ball suspended in time and space and the keeper in the background, still fumbling to get back to guard her goalmouth. Thembi cocks back her leg and then, without mercy, pulls the trigger. The goalkeeper feels the ball more than she sees it. Like the swish of a comet that just misses the earth, the ball brushes past her face and flies into the top corner of the net.

The apps are closed, the flashes are out, and the fans are on their feet as they whistle and cheer and try to pronounce the name "Kgatlana". It is a difficult name for a Chinese tongue. The closest they get to Thembi is "Sangbi", a name that sticks. The clock has run its course. The fans keep chanting "Sangbi! Sangbi!" Thembi's teammates run to embrace her, fully, for the first time, forever grateful that she has rescued this game for them. Thembi kisses her hand and then bends down and touches the strap on her ankle, grateful for the skilled Dutch physiotherapist in her life who transformed her twisted ankle from a moonboot filler to a game finisher.

CHAPTER 32

The Jamaica Incident

During a training session in Beijing one day, Thembi receives the news that she has been called upon by her country to play an international friendly against Jamaica. Her club coach is hesitant. He has seen her potential and is not keen to play without her. He worries that she might get injured on some dodgy field playing internationally in Africa. On top of this, Beijing Phoenix has qualified for the Chinese Women's Cup quarter finals, and Thembi has played an instrumental role in getting them there, even scoring a goal in the game before. The coach is devastated at the prospect of not having his tricky South African attacker for the final. For Thembi though, it is not a debate. The call has been sent, and she intends to answer. Thembi and Linda fly three hours to Hong Kong, and then 12 hours to OR Tambo International. They land on a Sunday morning, and the team is due to camp in Durban the next evening. Jetlag smashes Thembi like a hammer. Her lids droop low, her mind is still six hours behind her body.

The next morning, before the birds are even awake, there is a van waiting outside for Thembi. It has been organised by Nike. Thembi is needed at a photoshoot in Soweto before she can jet off to Durban. The shoot would include a few of the Banyana Banyana girls – but also girls dreaming of being in Banyana Banyana. Young and full of hope, but short on opportunity. Although Thembi wears exhaustion on her face, there is something inside her that comes alive when she interacts with these young girls, when she sees the look in their eyes. Thembi encourages them, but she knows that most of them won't make it, and it breaks her heart. Thembi decides there and then that someday soon, she will make a difference in these girls' lives.

That evening, Thembi is on the short flight. The plane doors open to another humid, sticky, serene evening in tropical Durban. Reuniting with her Banyana Banyana teammates is like coming home to family. But there is something different this time, a level of focus that can be felt between the players. All of them have, at the back of their minds, the upcoming World Cup. They know that every step they take from here on out is geared towards that.

On the evening before the game against Jamaica, an unusual event is organised – the players from both teams have dinner together. It is not common for warring nations to break bread the night before a battle, but here Thembi finds herself, in a bus on the way to uShaka Marine World to meet the Reggae Girlz.

Both Jamaica and South Africa are lively nations, full of passion and rhythm. The players bond easily, laugh quickly and realise that they have lots in common. After the dinner, the two teams say goodnight to each other, excited to put on a good show for their fans the next day.

Thembi expects to play a full game. In her humble opinion, at this stage of her career, nobody can doubt that she is an incredible footballer. She has the accolades, the sponsors and the overseas club to show for it. Yet when the starting line-up is announced hers is not among the eleven names on the list.

Thembi once again goes to that place where she tells herself to be selfless. To park her ego and think of the team. She tries to create the same excitement she had in America, where she knew she only had 10 minutes to play but saw it as an opportunity rather than a limitation. She tries to remember the fans shouting, "It's Thembi time!" as the game neared its final kick. However, she is not in America, she is in Durban, sitting on a bench, half a world away from her club, which is currently playing for a medal.

Thembi cannot find the strength to be excited today. The deeper she digs for motivation, the more frustration she finds.

With precisely 10 minutes to go and the score locked at 1-1, Thembi is called up. She runs onto the field, but she just does not feel right. What follows is 10 of the most emotional minutes of her career. She just cannot get behind the ball, cannot find space, and cannot get that lump of sadness out of her throat.

I really wanted to play that game, the whole game. I wanted to test myself, to see how I had progressed since being in China. It was a long journey home, but what made it bearable was to imagine playing for my country again – to imagine moments of individual brilliance and the way I was going to dazzle my opponent. It was not to be, though – and that hurt. I played the worst 10 minutes of football I've ever played in my life.

Thembi boards the plane back to China. Unlike when she arrived in South Africa, she's in a foul mood. Back in China, she fights her way through the jetlag and, once again, by the time she reaches Beijing, she can barely keep her eyes open. Her coach is fuming. Beijing Phoenix lost the quarter final, and he makes sure to call a meeting with Thembi as soon as she steps inside the grounds. He lights one cigarette with the end of the previous one, keeping them on a smoky loop. Fumes seem to be coming out the top of his head. His face turns red as he paces up and down his office, shouting but never looking directly at Thembi: "How could they do this? How could they be so selfish? SAFA, your football organisation, is selfish. They disrupt our season, to fly you halfway around the world to play you for just 10 minutes? Where is the respect? For you, for me, for this club. If they knew that they weren't going to play you, they could have just left you right here."

Thembi shares his frustration. She too wanted that gold medal on her shelf. Both of them feel the empty devastation of a missed opportunity to gain another accolade.

It is a sign of challenges yet to come in 2019. Thembi quickly realises that it is a different ball game getting a handle on your emotions when you are far from home.

Strike a Rock

One thing I learnt from my dad is that, when the going gets tough, never complain, just trust yourself and move forward. Sometimes, something negative can spark a chain of positive things.

CHAPTER 33

This House Is Haunted

For the first time in Thembi's life, she has money saved. She spends a long time mulling over how it should get used. Some images briefly flash through her mind – fresh Nike kicks, the leather seats of a Bentley, the smooth edges of a Smeg fridge, or holidays in Mauritius. These are natural thoughts for any person with new money. However, there is one thought that she just cannot push from her head: her father. She imagines the pain he has had to bear, all these years staying in his wife's mother's house, the community gossip he has had to endure, the accusations of being less than a man, of being someone who has not provided his family with his own house, someone who "freeloads" off his wife's late mother. This thought bothers Thembi immensely, as she knows that anything her father has done has simply been for the purpose of keeping his family together.

A year before, Thembi paid for some minor renovations to the family home on Mohapi Street. She got a new roof installed, one that does not leak. She got new tiles put in, ones without cracks. She replaced the window frames Tumelo took during that drug binge. Thembi hoped this would bring her parents some comfort and stop the community gossip. However, it only made it worse.

"Who do these people think they are?" the people asked. "Renovating a house that is not theirs? Shame on them. What would their mother say if she were alive? Seeing her home getting messed with by people who never bought it in the first place?"

So Thembi quickly pushes the Nike kicks and Bentley seats from her mind. She realises that renovating a house haunted by pain is much like putting makeup on a beast. Regardless of what you do on the outside, the soul of the beast remains. Thembi phones her parents one day and asks where they would like to live. The question confuses them. "We already have a house," they say.

Thembi purchases a stand in the outskirts of Mohlakeng, and a building contractor comes to visit her parents. This confuses them even more. They can't afford to build a house, they tell her. Her parents do not know how much money she makes. In her father's head, it is impossible for a woman footballer to earn build-a-new-house kind of money. Thembi finds their concerns endearing and funny,

"I don't want you guys to worry about money," she tells them. "I just want you to think about how you would like your dream house to look, and tell the contractor that."

The blueprints pass back and forth between South Africa and China. When Thembi accepts the plans, and the spade first breaks ground in early January 2019, it is the first time Thembi can hand a set of keys to her parents, for a house of their own. She knows that the feeling of handing over these keys is more soul-filling than the feeling of sliding into a new pair of kicks, while her parents languish in their haunted home. She hopes it will be a house of peace, a house of love.

CHAPTER 34

My Success Is Our Success

With every passing day, Thembi is changing. She is not just becoming a different athlete, but a different human too. Her name is spoken in corners of the globe that she has never heard of. On Instagram, next to the handle @kgatlanathe1st, there is a sparkling blue tick. For those who might not know, the blue tick is the official badge of fame on a social media account. It means you are well known enough, have gained so many thousands of followers, and are famous enough that people make parody accounts in your name. So Instagram needs to call you up to make sure this account is really run by you.

Another thing Thembi is also experiencing for the first time is being well paid. Her one-year contract with her Chinese club is coming to an end. And as she sits on the plane back East, she thinks about her newfound fame and wealth, and how it should be used. Thembi knows that she has to play it carefully. The history of South African football is littered with the crushed dreams of once-rich, once-famous, washed-up players. It is a short career, and after fame, when times are dark, friends are indeed, very few. Thembi thinks about the word "legacy". She rolls it around in her mouth, considering its meaning and implications. She takes out a notepad and starts jotting down some thoughts. She knows this is a vision she will have to craft and polish over some time. She knows that her most important responsibility though is to her current employer, the one who allows her to dream. She knows that she wants to leave a legacy in China too. There are only a handful of games left of the season, and she wants to make sure that the People's Republic speaks about the little South African rocket for years after she has left.

For the last game of 2019, Phoenix is playing a good team, Changchun Zhuoyue, away from home. They hold the ball well and pass it even better. Earlier in the season, Beijing Phoenix had been walloped by this team. Thembi was out with an injury at the time. Injury is the curse of the professional athlete, the menacing fog that prevents true potential from being reached. Thembi feels that her earlier injury has cost her precious time. She knows that this final game of the season is her last shot at paving any kind of legacy here.

In the early minutes of the Changchun game, the ball gets played over the centre of the field and bounces in the opposition half. Thembi runs side by side with the defender. She holds up her opposite number but then, right before they reach the bouncing ball, Thembi sticks out her arm and muscles the defender out of the way before taking the shot. She sends a bullet train straight into the back of the net. Beijing Phoenix takes the lead.

Dizzy with euphoria, the Phoenix players go into a lull and, before long, Changchun has equalised. During the next counter attack, Thembi puts in a slick pass to set up Phoenix's second goal, and they're ahead again. The relentless Changchun comes back with another equaliser.

In the second half, Thembi fires in her team's third goal, and once again they edge ahead. But once again, the joy is short lived as the enemy equalises yet again, towards the end of the match. With the final seconds dripping away and the whistle nestled between the referee's lips, Thembi puts in yet another pin-point pass and assists the final goal. Beijing Phoenix win the match 4-3. It is the kind of game that will not be forgotten anytime soon. And Thembi is the kind of player who will not be forgotten in any kind of a rush either.

On the plane back to South Africa after the end of the season in

China, Thembi smiles. She leans back, puts her feet up, crosses her hands behind her head, and she smiles. Thembi knows she gave a good account of herself in the East, and she has been rewarded for it. Once again, she starts thinking of the word "legacy." She puts her hand up, and two flight attendants come running.

"One more orange juice, please."

They giggle like children, "Yes, Miss Kgatlana."

As she watches the clouds gallop past the airplane window, she realises that she is, for the first time in her life, in a position where her actions could have a real impact.

The Thembi Kgatlana Foundation is registered towards the end of 2019. The slogan licks a cool *"my success, our success"* in gold lettering under the logo. It is almost expected of a footballer to give back in some way, given how handsomely they are paid. The thing is, many footballers are only able to pay mere lip service: visit an underprivileged school, take a photograph and post it on social media. Although any effort for charity is a welcomed one, Thembi wants her impact to last longer than that. She wants a legacy cast in stone, an initiative that can make a genuine difference in the life of the South African girl child.

SUNDAY FOOTBALL IN SOUTH AFRICA is unlike anything else. All across the country, on dusty fields from Musina to Mohlakeng, football comes alive. Sunday kasi tournaments are the lifeblood of the sport in the country. Festivities begin in the morning, with teams travelling from nearby areas to compete. Food and clothes are sold along the embankments. In the mornings, the crowd is thin but undeniably present. As the day grows older, the stream of humans filling up the spaces around the field grows thicker.

On television, South Africa's professional league teams – big name clubs – play to a procession of empty plastic chairs in giant, empty, once-loved stadiums. And yet, on a Sunday, you drive to these stadiums in the townships on the outskirts of the cities, and you see a different world entirely. Hundreds – if not thousands – of fans cram in. There's not a phone in sight; all eyes are on the field. The fans are as much a part of the game as the players, shooting whistles of approval onto the field, or blanketing it with a disapproving hum when play gets a little dry. You see, the football played in a South African township on a Sunday is different to the football on TV, and it is much more loved. Stadium football places a high premium on rigorous tactics, crisp passes, tactical goals and cohesive teamwork. Kasi football has an entirely different set of values. The emphasis is on attitude. The goal is entertainment. Individual flair is supreme, and style is non-negotiable. On a township pitch on a Sunday, you will see something not seen in other nations around the world. You will see a country that has redefined football for itself.

The country is not short on these local football tournaments; they occur throughout the year. Some are more professional than others. There is one very pale element to them though – all of the tournaments are set up for the purposes of men's football. Every now and then a women's team will be invited to participate, but it is the exception and not the norm.

So one day in 2017, Thembi has a thought. This thought grows over the months, takes different shapes until eventually, that thought becomes something impactful. The Thembi Kgatlana Tournament dedicates itself to accelerating women's football in the country. Consisting of 10 women's teams, this football festival is held in Thembi's heartland – Mohlakeng. The news of the country's first all-women football tournament spreads like mist in the air, reaching the ears of ambitious women from all over the country. Buses file in from Limpopo, Mpumalanga, the Western Cape. When the players depart, they are focused yet thrilled. This tournament will also not pass by in blur on a Sunday afternoon; the Thembi Kgatlana Tournament is a four-day celebration of women's football. Thembi rallies her corporate sponsors, and the event is well supported.

I didn't do this for me. I didn't even do this for my community. I did this to send a message to the South African girl child – we can do this.

What is also of serious importance to Thembi is the outcome. Women athletes should be rewarded for their talent and professionalism, just like their male peers. So Thembi organises prizes, she organises money for the winners, real money. She organises trophies and cheques for the player of the tournament, the top goal scorer, the best goalkeeper and so on. Thembi then personally buys all of the players new football boots.

I know what it is like. Some of these players are professional, but they do not get paid. So they cannot afford new boots. How is a player ever going to compete at an international level if she can't even get the right boots? It is not even about the boots. I just want to show them that they are appreciated, that somebody sees them, that somebody recognises their hard work.

Thembi suspects that it will be an overwhelming feeling, being at this tournament with her name on it. When she stands on the side of the field though, she finds herself wholly unprepared for the surge of emotion that charges through her body. Thembi looks out over the field and she sees a haven. It is almost surreal, being in the heart of Mohlakeng – the place where her football upbringing was spent, jostling with a field full of boys. Thembi sees what is possible if the girl child is protected. That is all that it takes for women to flourish, just the freedom to be. Thembi looks out over the fields, she sees divine potential, she sees girls smiling, making friends, competing with one another. She takes a look at the river of talent she has assembled. Thembi is lost in her thoughts, thinking about how all of this came from just a single idea in her mind, and the will to help. A little girl tugs at Thembi's shirt. Thembi looks around and then down at the little girl.

"Hello, little one."

"Hello, Thembi."

The little girl is shy. Thembi bends down and talks to her on her level.

"Are you okay, little one?"

"Yes… It's just that I… I have always dreamt of meeting you."

Thembi has a thought right then that sticks with her: *As heroes, we need to make ourselves available.*

The Thembi Kgatlana Foundation does not exist for profit. So all leftover cash from the sponsors is earmarked for good causes.

I know girls whose parents can't afford sanitary pads and they have to go to school and have to use whatever they can find. Imagine a girl trying to make it as a professional athlete, having to go to training and play sport while she is on her period, and nobody in her life can afford sanitary products. The second you give a girl a sanitary pad, she can go to school, she can go to training, she can live.

Thembi and her foundation identify four high schools in the area where they hand out sanitary pads. Next they identify a handful of primary schools and buy school shoes for the learners. The smiling students are then all equipped with bright, shiny and new stationery as the foundation hands out 1 200 pencil cases.

Thembi then buys 100 new soccer balls. She remembers growing up on these streets, and how the boys would not always let the girls join them for a game, so it is important to Thembi to hand out the new footballs to both boys and girls. She drives around her old hood and stops when she sees a group of children playing. She loves talking to the kids, asking about their dreams and their life before rolling the new football over to them and driving on.

You want these kids to dream. You want them to walk straight past what society expects of them.

CHAPTER 35

The Eagles of Portugal

Thembi's plan has always been to return to China. Although she has left her mark in the East, she believes that there is always more to be done. Thembi bathes in the sunshine and happiness that characterises the South African December while she waits on an email from China. Thembi is not sweating one drop though; text messages from China keep her spirit high: "Just hang tight, Thembi. We are busy sorting contract details. We would hope and love to have you back. – Director, Beijing."

Around the same time, Thembi's agent lets her know about an additional deal on the table. The number one team in China likes what they saw of the little South African last season, and they have put some numbers on the table. The contract is printed, the ink is still wet, all that awaits are the curves of Thembi's signature.

"What do you want to do?" Thembi's agent asks.

"Let's wait," Thembi responds calmly.

The call is to give Beijing Phoenix the chance to at least put a deal on the table. Thembi is a strong subscriber to the principles of loyalty, and given the love, support and warmth shown to her by Beijing Phoenix, she thinks it is only fair to allow them to make an offer for her services before they refuse them.

And so they wait. And the days on the calendar tick on. And Thembi's agent finds himself shifting in his desk chair uncomfortably and rolling from side to side in bed at night, caught in a web of thoughtful worry.

One night, at around 9.30pm, Thembi's phone screen lights up. Her agent's number flashes to the beat of the ringtone.

Thembi taps the green button, "Who died?"

"Huh? Ah, good evening Thembi,"

"Evening indeed, dude, I am about to sleep, so tell me who died, so I can get on with it."

"No one died, Thembi, but I have a spanner to throw at you. We have a new contract offer, and it is not from either of the two teams in China."

"Well, who is this new team?"

"The team is Sporting Lisbon Benfica, from Portugal."

"Sporting what from where? Who are these people now?"

"SL Benfica, Thembi, one of the oldest and proudest institutions in men's football anywhere in the world. They have only recently founded their women's team. They want to go all the way to the top. They want to invest in the future of women's football, Thembi, they want to invest in you. This thing is real. Playing in Europe is the goal for any footballer. Now is your chance."

Thembi listens to her agent as she nods her head slowly, pacing up and down the room, digesting the news in front of the late night flashing television screen. Thembi hears the desperate excitement in her agent's voice; it cracks like the vocals of a child on the verge of convincing their parents to buy a puppy. Thembi eventually offers an answer: "That is exciting. I hear you. Still, I think we should wait."

Thembi spends the next few days getting reabsorbed into her community, visiting old friends and going for morning runs accompanied by an army of children from the area. Her agent spends this time nervously, refreshing his emails every five minutes and then massaging the temples of his head when he sees nothing new and unopened from China. Meanwhile, his inbox floods with messages from Portugal. They too need only a signature from Thembi, and from then, all that is required from her is to not miss her flight to Lisbon. Two days later Thembi's phone glows up again in the late dark hours of the evening. It can only be her agent at this hour.

"Who died?"

"Thembi, *we* might die if we don't sign this contract. While we are waiting for Beijing to offer us a contract, the transfer window is closing. Soon there won't be enough space in that window for us to slip through and find you a new club to play for. You will spend the next season of your life playing Sunday league football in Mohlakeng. You won't be able to keep up your foundation. I know we had planned to return to China, but in life plans do change, and I think it's time you take on a new challenge. Let's go to Europe. Let's test ourselves against the world's best, let's just see what happens?"

On 23 January 2020, Thembi Kgatlana boards a plane from Johannesburg to Lisbon, Portugal. Thembi is completely surprised by the warmth with which the Portuguese accept her. From the airport to the stadium, she is welcomed by banners, posters and singing supporters.

There is one slight issue though. In order for Thembi to officially become a Benfica player, she requires a release form from her previous club in China. Without this form, Thembi cannot register for the season. Getting hold of the document is no easy task. Thembi's former club is not exactly incentivised to hand it over in any kind of a rush. As far as they are concerned, this is a favour for a player who rejected them. The sporting director at Benfica rolls the dice on Thembi and tells the coach that he should start training with Thembi. He has faith that it will all be sorted come game day.

Benfica's first game of the season is coming up. It's against SC Braga, a powerhouse in Portuguese women's football. The game is a four-hour bus trip up north from Lisbon. They leave the day before the game. Thembi steps onto the bus in her Benfica tracksuit. She is still not officially a player. The coach, the directors and Thembi's teammates all feel the discomfort of the situation. They are gearing up for a cracker of a season opener against the league's best, and they want to know if they can use their new

African weapon in the fight.

Meanwhile back in South Africa, the six-hour time difference with China wreaks havoc on Thembi's agent's insomnia, but it also gives him the extra hours he needs to really ramp up the efforts of nagging Beijing Phoenix to release Thembi. The next day, when Benfica kick off against Braga will also be the last day of the transfer window. If Thembi does not have her documentation in line by then, then the African Women Footballer of the Year will spend the season as an amateur, telling people how she almost made it in Europe.

Thembi usually does not have any issues in falling asleep. However, as dawn sneaks over the Portuguese horizon and the birds whistle their morning melody, Thembi Kgatlana lies perfectly still with her eyes open staring at the ceiling. Her eyes have been open the whole night. She has run over the situation in her head a million times. How could the rest of her career depend entirely on a piece of paper from China? Her phone rattles off of the bedside table. It is not a phone call from her agent. It is an alarm, and Thembi crawls her way out of bed towards the breakfast buffet downstairs.

Thembi is busy serving herself her second helping of eggs when she notices a large Portuguese man approaching her at an alarming pace. He has strong eyebrows, a massive moustache and an even bigger smile. Thembi puts down her plate but holds onto the serving spoon, as a weapon, just in case. The big Portuguese man extends his arms out sideways and continues pacing towards her. When he reaches her, he wraps his big Portuguese arms around Thembi, lifts her off her feet and squeezes her and the serving spoon tight while swinging her from left to right in a passionate bear hug.

"Thembi, we did it!"

He puts her back down. The big excitable Portuguese man in front of her is the director of the club.

"Your clearance came through from China this morning. This is great news for this club, this is great news for the people of this city. You can play in the game tonight Thembi, *vamos*!"

The match is due to kick off at 7.30pm. The sky grumbles and moans through darkening clouds; rain and wind thrash the city into waterlogged misery. For the suspicious, the weather is a bad omen. For the practical, it is an inconvenience. It favours no one. Thembi's nerves intensify while she watches rain bead down a window pane. She knows that while others get to remain warm inside, she must go battle in the elements.

To make conditions more conducive to the fluttering of the butterflies in Thembi's stomach, she begins the game on the bench. Although she is used to it, she never enjoys starting on the bench, for no other reason but that she finds her nerves are exponentially more jittery. She has actually come to realise that she is an unpleasant person to sit next to on the bench. She cannot sit still, and her leg shakes uncontrollably, neverendingly. It is for this reason that Thembi always tries to sit at the end of the bench, so that the side of the booth takes the brunt of her nervous energy, and her teammates can focus on the game without having to tell her to settle down.

SC Braga score the first goal. It is disappointing for Benfica but not altogether surprising. They are the clear underdogs in this fixture. SC Braga have been the national bully in recent years, dominating many other teams in the league, sometimes with brutal scores. Benfica are new to the league.

After the first goal, the stadium erupts like a shaken soft drink bottle. Thembi jumps from her seat. She realises something that has been in front of her face this whole time, that she just has not paid attention to yet. The stadium is full. Really full. Thembi only knows playing in front of crowds like this during the Olympics or World Cup. The crowd is not only full, but it is fiery, it is hostile. Thembi loves it. This is the kind of passion that should be poured over women's football all over the world.

Just before halftime the captain of Benfica equalises, and they go into the changerooms with their tails slightly up. Around the 55th minute, Thembi's coach sends a subtle nod in her direction. She understands the instruction, laces up her boots and starts her warm-up on the side of the field. She notices the fans noticing her. They point at her, whisper into each other's ears, take out their phones and search for her online. Thembi shakes and stretches the last bit of rust out of her legs. She stands on the side-lines and gives one final spring up into the air. She feels fresh. On the 65th minute, the referee signals that she can join the game.

Before Thembi's came onto the field, the match was a tense but civilised one. Structure versus structure, neither team daring to venture on too exotic of an attack. There was order. Clean passing. Honest shooting. Up until this point, it had been a football game played in the spirit of chess. As soon as Thembi's foot crosses the chalk line though, an element of madness enters the game. Her runs seem to disorientate even her own teammates. She is showing hints of impossible energy and speed, getting in behind defenders and enticing the screaming opposition coach on the side-line to quickly think of alternative tactics.

The momentum of play has undoubtedly swung, and within 10 minutes of her arrival, Thembi has already planted the ball in the back of the net. As she turns to celebrate though, she sees the menacing snitch of a linesman's flag sticking high in the air like an unwanted red pimple. Offside, they say. Thembi shrugs it off. She knows she is not yet done. Her opposition knows she is far from finished. Thembi zips between defenders and taunts the opposition goal like a fox circling a nest full of chicken eggs.

Thembi rounds two defenders on the wing and finds herself dangerously close to the opposition. She tears through another dozen metres, and now she is in the box. Four defenders form a fort around her. Thembi pings the ball off of one of their legs and forces the corner. The set piece is taken quickly, a handsome cross floats into the box and is headed home by one of the midfielders. Benfica go ahead 2-1.

SC Braga wear a look of collective shock. They refocus their efforts entirely on Thembi. Their defensive attempts are fruitless though, and in the 85th minute Thembi gets the assist for the final goal. Benfica run out 3-1 victors.

On the drive back to Lisbon, Thembi's teammates surround her, asking her questions about where she is from and how she learnt to play football. They put their chins on their crossed arms and they listen like children around a campfire. The bus rolls on for the four hours until they reach Lisbon.

WHAT STRIKES THEMBI THE most about Portugal is the level to which people mind their own business. That suits her just fine. She is from a place where minding one's own business is highly regarded. So she minds her own business too. The team has put her in an apartment not far from the stadium. It is fairly high up and has a breath-stopping view looking at rolling hills of waving trees. The big window in Thembi's room looks like a painting, as it looks out onto splashes of red, orange and green. Close to her apartment is a zoo. Thembi loves the zoo. She loves the intimacy with the animals, the connection she feels when she looks in their eyes. Sometimes, on her off days, she goes to the zoo straight from breakfast, and she stays there until a security guard comes and says, "*Perdon, senorita.*"

Then she knows it is time to go. She bids the rhinos good night and the owls good day and she heads off home to dream about the animals. One time Thembi sits and watches a pride of four lions sleeping for five hours. Thembi's favourite animal is the tiger.

The tiger always knows what it wants. The tiger is resilient. The tiger is underestimated. Everyone knows what a lion can do, but not everyone knows, really knows, the strength of the tiger. When I look at a tiger, I feel like I am looking at myself. I get my style from the tiger. I sleep like the tiger. I hunt like the tiger.

The zoo in Lisbon has four different types of tigers: Sumatran, Bengal, Malayan and White.

SL Benfica have a beautiful emblem featuring a proud eagle. The club itself is more than 100 years old. In order to honour their badge, the club has actual eagles that live in the stadium. They are bald eagles, and there are three of them. The main two are named Vitória and Gloria (victory and glory).

The eagles sleep behind the home goalpost inside the stadium. When the players train, the eagles watch over them. Occasionally, their handler stumbles down to a practice session and trains his birds alongside the team. On weekdays, one of the eagles is posted up in the club shop, fascinating tourists and frightening children. The third and oldest eagle is a little moody, so he is released from official club duty and can just spend his days watching the players train.

The main purpose of the eagles is to act as the team's spiritual forklift, to lift the mood and infect the players with bravery just before kick-off. On game day, as the teams are about to face off, the trainer will stand on the roof of the stadium, with Vitória proudly perched on his gloved forearm. The trainer always sets his legs wide apart, taking a power stance, like the silhouette of a villain in a doorway in a movie. He gives a sharp blast of the whistle nestled in his mouth. The eagle takes off and circles the stadium. Vitória has a number of ribbons tied to her feet, red and white to represent the colours of the club. When she flies, the ribbons stream and wave behind her in the wind. It is a glorious sight, one that usually sends the crowd into a hypnotic frenzy. Vitória sweeps over the stadium, swooping and ducking through the thick atmosphere and shouting fans on game day. Once she has blessed the stadium with her victory lap, she lands on a podium placed in the centre circle of the field. It is only after this that the game can commence.

The club goes a long way to make sure that Thembi not only knows the club's history, but that she *understands* it. They hand her the number 11 jersey. She is informed that she is the first woman to ever don that number at the club. They walk her through the halls of the museum, pointing to stained and grainy black-and-white photos, pausing to commemorate the legends and then pointing to the empty space next to the picture where they hope Thembi's frame will one day appear.

Thembi is hitting her stride with Benfica. She is immediately liked by her teammates for her spirited personality and how it bubbles over into the changeroom. She is adored by the fans for her style, ease and trickery, and she is feared by the opposition for her ability to ruthlessly attack until the other team is beaten to submission.

Thembi enjoys life in Portugal, feeling mature as a footballer and a human. She trains hard and plays even harder, and a few days off to rest are welcomed by all the players. Thembi only thinks of going to one place – back to the animals.

While Thembi watches the tigers stroll gracefully around their enclosures, she thinks about life and all the potential that her future holds. She tries to script the different paths she might take and where she could end up when her playing days are over. Of all the events that Thembi forecasts in her head, there is one that she has no way of predicting.

While Thembi is philosophising, there is a man getting sick, 10 000 kilometres away in a place called Wuhan. Soon enough, another man gets sick. Not long after that, scores of people all over the world begin to fall ill. The zoo locks up. The footballs get packed away, fear sweeps the streets, and Thembi retreats to her little apartment in the sky.

At the time that the league gets cancelled, SL Benfica are at the top of the log. This has the even brighter implication that they stand a good chance of making the UEFA Champions League, the holy grail of European club football. For Thembi, the national lockdown is as confusing and scary as it is for anyone else. Thembi also cannot get home. South Africa has taken a no-nonsense approach to its closure, and anyone stuck outside of the country after April stays outside. Thembi has a greater grasp on what she does not want out of lockdown than what she does. She knows one thing she does not want is to become lazy. She already has a naturally lazy person inside her, waiting to be stirred from her afternoon nap. She knows unless she works against it, the lazy person inside will take over. Thembi keeps up the home training, starting every day with a sweat, making sure she makes the most of the 10 square metres that she is now confined to. Further than just exercise though, Thembi also recognises the lockdown as an opportunity to work on the mind, so she begins to read.

Thembi does not just read, she devours books. Gobbling up individual words, letting them swirl in her mouth before digesting them. She gets lost in the paragraphs, dances between the sentences, and finds a piece of herself in the middle of the lonely full stop that gets inked at the end of every line.

She has a particular penchant for the stories of successful people. She gets lost in the tales of Phil Knight, Michael Jordan and Teko Modise. The book on Michael Jordan has a particular impact on Thembi. She realises how family shapes the life of a successful person. Whether it's hurting or helping, it's still shaping. It makes Thembi think about her brother Tumelo back home, a sweet boy by nature, who is now blanketed in a cloud of wrongdoing. Thembi thinks about Tumelo's personality. He has redeeming qualities, and there is something about his smile that gives a little preview to the potential of his soul, a kind of charm that makes it difficult to hate him. However, as Thembi thinks more about him, and all that he has put the family through, she realises that the greatest motivation she can draw from her brother is the desire to never end up like him.

Thembi reads a story one day, and for some or other reason it sticks with her. The story involves a family sitting down for dinner. They hear a noise outside and they exit the house to investigate. As they stand on their lawn, they feel a warmth on their backs and hear a crackling in their ears. The family turns around to see their home on fire. The wife suggests that this is the most devastating thing that could happen to them. The husband urges her to look around, notice their children, feel their breath, take note of the fact that they are still alive. For if they are still alive, there is still hope, and as long as there is hope, there is no devastation.

Thembi has a lot of time to do interviews during the lockdown. Without fail, almost every single journalist asks her how she stays so positive in the face of such uncertainty. She often cannot find the exact right words to answer the question, but in her mind she has a picture of a burning house, a family standing on a lawn and a story about hope.

In the middle of the lockdown, with infection numbers spiking all around Thembi and morgues filling up, she receives an email from Benfica. It is the kind of email one hopes to never receive from one's employer. They ask if Thembi's available for a chat. From the tone of the mail, it sounds like it will be a difficult talk.

The director of the club sits on the other side of the video call.

He looks down at his papers nervously and rearranges them for the fifth time since the meeting started. He can barely look his computer camera directly in the eye.

"Thembi, we have got some difficult news. Obviously, nobody saw this coming. Nobody knew there was going to be a global pandemic this year. We have to look at our club, and we have to recognise that the survival of Benfica is the most important thing. We all have to make sacrifices. And it is for this reason that we are requesting you and your teammates to take a salary cut."

"Does this apply to everyone?"

"As I said, Thembi, we all have to make sacrifices."

"Are the men also taking a salary cut?"

"Thembi, there are things you must understand. This is a pandemic. Every company everywhere in the world is having to make sacrifices."

"I understand the pandemic. I understand sacrifice. I am asking you if the men in this team also have to take a salary cut."

"Not yet, no."

"So it is just the women who must take a pay cut?"

"Right now, yes."

"Okay. I will make this very easy for you then. You don't have to cut my salary. In fact, you don't have to pay me at all. I will be leaving."

It is a big call for Thembi to make. Definitely not the safe option. To leave your employer in the middle of a pandemic is a bold move, even if they promise to pay you less than half of what you earned before. Thembi, however, has a bigger picture in mind.

We often get too scared in life. Particularly when it comes to jobs and making decisions on our future. I felt that if I were to stay at Benfica and accept the salary cut, it would be an injustice. Not just a personal injustice, but an injustice against all the women who will come after me. The decisions I take can set a precedent for them. Sometimes in life, it is all about money, but there are situations where dignity is more important than money. It starts with knowing your worth. After you recognise your worth, you can be loyal to yourself. Remind yourself of what you have been through to get to this point in your life. I personally know that I have worked hard to earn what I earn, and I will not allow anyone to reduce me, especially if the reason for me being reduced is the fact that I am a woman. I felt I had to take a stand for all women everywhere. I felt I had to set the example of being loyal to myself.

CHAPTER 36

I Tell My Daughter About You

Thembi is in Mohlakeng with her parents in May 2019, feasting at a buffet, when suddenly a television in the corner of the restaurant is turned louder. The patrons stop eating and turn to focus on the screen, the waiter stops working and holds the remote limply in his hand. The news anchor wears an emotionless mask on his face as he announces the Banyana Banyana squad that will be going to France to compete in the team's first ever World Cup.

When Thembi's name is announced, chaos ensues. The restaurant turns into a hive of joy, forks slam down onto plates, and Thembi's family are on their feet, jumping with unfiltered excitement. They have not felt joy like this since Thembi aced her matric results.

Thembi is overwhelmed with the wave of congratulations that wash over her. She walks around her community and humbly accepts the praise, yet she is nervous. Her ankle is still giving her trouble, and she hopes that she will have the strength to play through any pain that may come.

Thembi walks past the field that she used to play on as a child. She finds herself alone with a quiet moment. She reflects on her football upbringing, and how she used to battle on this gravel, being the only girl in a field of boys. They did not play soft when they went up against Thembi. At times it was brutal, but ultimately it made her tougher. Thembi remembers the feeling of being up against Goliath, and being thrilled by the challenge. Thembi looks over the pitch and thinks forward to the World Cup. She is about to do something that South African women do not get to do often. In fact, it is something that no South African woman has ever done before.

She realises that she is made of tougher stuff than most others out there. She realises that whether her ankle niggles with pain or not, any pain she feels will be kept internal. She intends to stand before Goliath in France, and show no fear in her body.

Thembi is inundated with congratulations and praise following the announcement of her selection to the World Cup squad. Thembi's name is more famous than her face, and she finds this often puts her in awkward positions. As part of her congratulations, the television presenter Carol Tshabalala tells Thembi that she has organised a gift for her from England. Thembi's footballing icon is Liverpool star Sadio Mané. Carol is well aware of this, and also enjoys a close personal friendship with Sadio himself. She organises a signed Liverpool jersey from the Senegalese star, addressed to Thembi. When Carol returns home with the jersey, she leaves it at the offices of Multichoice, the owners of the station she presents for. With the jersey, Carol leaves a simple note – "For Banyana Banyana star Thembi Kgatlana x."

At the Multichoice office, she tells the security guard who she is and why she's there. The guard squints her eyes in suspicion. She scans Thembi from head to toe. She sees a girl dressed in loose-fitting clothes and a hat pulled down low. She does not sense anything celebrity-like about Thembi. The security guard hesitantly fetches the jersey. An awkward few minutes follow. The security guard clutches the jersey closer to her chest, refusing to hand it over.

"Are you sure you are Thembi Kgatlana?"

Thembi laughs her hearty laugh before pulling out her phone, googling her own name and turning the screen to show the guard her Wikipedia page. The guard grudgingly hands over the jersey. When Thembi exits the building and starts descending the steps, she looks back over her shoulder to see the security guard still standing there, with her hands on her hips, still suspiciously watching her, not fully believing that she has just met a star.

There is an unusual buzz about South Africa. There has not been much good news to print in the headlines. The story of the national women's team qualifying for their first ever World Cup is highly welcomed. Citizens everywhere reach out and grab the good news story. They bathe in it, and they spread it like pollen. Thembi has a profound feeling of depth in the days leading up to her departure for France. She feels herself infected with the spirit of the land, the hope of her people. She sees it in their eyes. This is a country in desperate need of new heroes.

With five days left until the plane leaves for Paris, Thembi is sent to fetch her uncle from the airport. Thembi looks cool in the driver's seat, comfortable, her Nikes fitting the pedals just right, her hat pulled down low and her elbow resting on the window. There are no issues except for the blinking petrol light on the dashboard.

"Up ahead, there is a Sasol Garage, let's pull in," Thembi's uncle says, yawning from the energy-sapping airport experience.

Thembi flicks the indicator and pulls in. Beyond filling Thembi's petrol tank today, Sasol is also the technical sponsor of Banyana Banyana. As such, they are running a promotion in the build-up to the World Cup. The petrol attendant approaches the car. Around his neck hangs a lanyard and at the end of that lanyard is a picture of the Banyana Banyana squad.

"Heita, hola," the petrol attendant greets Thembi and her uncle.

"Hello, please can you fill up, unleaded."

Thembi's uncle looks like he is on a sofa in the lounge. He is casual, cool, in no rush to be anywhere. He rolls a toothpick around in the corner of his mouth while he stares at the lanyard. A mischievous smile creeps onto his cheeks. He reaches out and pulls the petrol attendant by his shirt sleeve, bringing him closer to his window.

"Hey, my brother, do you know this team?" he asks, lifting the laminated picture on the lanyard.

"Of course I do. This is our team, brother. Have you seen these girls play? They are something special, I'm telling you. This team is better than Bafana Bafana."

Thembi's uncle releases a deep-bellied laugh, "Yes, I have seen them play, indeed they are a very strong team. But now I want to know, do you know any of these players?"

The attendant, halfway through cleaning the windscreen, drops his cloth and looks at the uncle, almost as if he is mildly offended by the question,

"Do I know the players? Of course I do. I like the goalkeeper, she is solid. I also like Captain Janine, she is strong. But there is one player, I have never seen a player like that in my life before. Her name is Thembi Kgatlana. Hey, that girl is something else. The ball just sticks to her feet. She is so fast, so skilful, so fierce."

Thembi remains silent, staring ahead, while her uncle nods his head slowly, almost as if to give the impression that it is his first time hearing her name spoken.

"That is interesting, my brother. And do you know where this Thembi girl comes from?

"Yes, my brother, Hammanskraal." He says with confidence, although he is about 130 kilometre from the truth.

"Interesting. Interesting. And let me ask you, if you ever had to meet this Thembi Kgatlana woman, what would you do?"

The attendant laughs and rolls his head back, almost as if the question is too silly to even be asked.

"My brother, if I met Thembi Kgatlana, I would go crazy. I would take pictures just to show to my children. They know, I talk about her all the time. I talk about Thembi all the time to show my daughter that she can be anything she wants to be. I don't even want to know what I would do if I ever got to meet Thembi."

Thembi's uncle slaps the dashboard and belts out a few more choruses of laughter before wrapping his hand around the petrol attendant's arm, pulling him down to the level of the car window. He looks at the attendant intensely for a second before pointing over his shoulder to his niece.

"Well, my man, today is your lucky day. This is Thembi Kgatlana sitting right next to me here."

The attendant's jaw involuntarily drops, his eyes dart from the uncle to Thembi. He is trying to figure out how he is being pranked. In the driver's seat, he just sees a small woman well hidden by her cap and shades. The attendant drops the heavy bunch of keys in his hand to the floor and runs around to the driver's side door. He bends down and opens the door, exposing a sitting, smiling Thembi Kgatlana.

He takes a deep breath and forces himself to calm down slightly.

"Excuse me, Ma'am. Please can you remove your cap quickly?"

Thembi takes off her cap and takes her shades off, placing them on her head. The attendant springs off the ground, punching both his fists into the air.

"Iyhooo!" He starts sprinting circles around the petrol station.

The other motorists look alarmed, his colleagues look concerned, as if this man has just lost his whole mind. He does two more laps around the station before stopping in front of Thembi's car, dropping to his knees, closing his eyes and pulling his hands together in prayer. Tears stream down his cheeks. He sobs heavily through his nose.

Thembi exits the car and walks up to him. She drops to her knees in front of him and wraps her arms around him. They hold each other for a few moments while a crowd gathers to see the commotion.

While the attendant is busy snapping enough selfies to show his children and their future children, other motorists exit their cars and approach Thembi,

"Hey, aren't you that Banyana Banyana star?"

"Wow, it is really you."

"You have no idea how much my daughter looks up to you."

Thembi spends an hour in the station, talking to all the fans, posing for pictures and signing pieces of paper for their children. It is a beautiful moment in Thembi's career, it is a beautiful moment for South Africa.

CHAPTER 37

Fearless in France

In June 2019, Thembi flies out to France a week before their first game, against Spain, to join the rest of the team in camp. As part of their preparations, Banyana Banyana play a warm-up friendly against Norway. It is a feisty affair, Banyana Banyana go for an all-out attack, leaving themselves exposed at the back. The result is a 5-2 loss. The score is more flattering than it seems; Banyana Banyana played a good game. Thembi wishes they could play again the next day, sure that they would win. But football is not kind enough to give second chances that easily. During the game, Thembi notices a delegation of Spanish technical staff, studying her closely and taking notes intensely. Thembi looks at them and learns something – she too needs to study herself. Studying your opponent goes without saying, but studying yourself requires you to break a certain mental barrier, to pull back a curtain and look into your deepest vulnerabilities. Most people are scared to take this step, afraid of what they might find, but Thembi realises that it may just be the key to her greatness. It is something Vera Pauw taught her – to always begin by acknowledging your weaknesses. So, leading up to the game against Spain, Thembi spends a lot of time on her laptop, watching clips of herself, rewinding, putting it into slow motion and watching again.

Thembi spends a lot of time watching clips of the Spanish team too.

I like to get to know my opponents' strengths as well as their weaknesses. If I know your strengths, I can get into your head. I will let you play to your strengths in the beginning, let you think that you are in control, and then when you least expect it, I will expose your weakness.

The more Thembi watches videos of the Spanish defence, the more she realises that none of them can match the pace she packs. Thembi licks her lips and rubs her hands.

Thembi cracks her eyelids open on the day before the opening game. She stares at the roof, she does not move her body, she does not feel right. There is a feeling that overwhelms her, it is not nerves, it is something beyond that. It sits heavy on her like a concrete blanket. Even the butterflies in her stomach have been scared back into their caves, inside she feels hollow anxiety. It is almost too much to bear. She closes her eyes again and tells herself to breathe before slowly getting out of bed.

At lunch, Thembi is quiet. It is unusual for her not to be at the centre of the team morale, and her stillness makes her teammates uneasy. Thembi is deep inside her own head, but it is in these recesses of her mind that she finds strength. Pain has always been a great motivator for her,

It is not a place you want me to be in, if you are against me. I think crazy things, and I find a lot of motivation in those dark spaces.

Thembi's nerves are palpable, they are contagious, and that night, her roommate Jermaine Seoposenwe cannot get even a moment's worth of sleep. The phone light shines bright against Jermaine's face, and she tries to make small talk with Thembi, attempting to entice her to stay awake with her teammate. Thembi grabs her pillow and, as she turns over to lie facing the other way, she says, "Hey, do what you gotta do. Me, I'm going to sleep."

The way Thembi sees it, any challenge tomorrow brings can be dealt with tomorrow, but one thing that cannot be taken back is a bad night's sleep. Thembi pops a muscle relaxer and is lightly snoring within two minutes of closing her eyes. At some point in the night, Thembi is awakened by the need to pee. She looks at the clock, it shines at 3am. She looks over to Jermaine's bed.

She sees the hypnotising glow of the phone screen lighting up her teammates face. Her eyes are wide open, and her thumb is aggressively scrolling through her timeline.

"You are crazy," Thembi says as she drifts across to the bathroom.

Dawn breaks the horizon on 8 June 2019. A French rooster calls out to the morning. The street lights turn off as the Le Havre skyline paints itself an ominous orange, suggesting that a battle will be fought today. Thembi Kgatlana wakes up. Jermaine and Thembi look at each other. They smile. They say nothing. Some occasions bring up a feeling beyond words.

Thembi usually stays off social media on the day of a match, but today she posts, "It's game day!" before logging off and putting her phone away. Thembi and Jermaine begin their usual game day rituals. They sing, they pray, they sing again, they create an environment charged with spirit. They create an environment of peace, a moment of calm.

Your body and mind will never operate better than when you are at peace.

Jermaine and Thembi are never without a speaker playing music. Usually it is Jermaine that must remember to bring hers, but this year, on Thembi's birthday, she bought her a speaker too, so that if one of them dies, the other can be powered up immediately, and they can ensure that there is never a moment of silence. On game day, overwhelming nerves fill the space that silence leaves.

Jermaine and Thembi are notorious for being late to breakfast. They often get so lost in the joy of their morning rituals that they do not notice the minutes getting swallowed up. They often get reprimanded by the team manager or one of the other players, and they often have to hurriedly defend themselves and reassure their teammates that they had not overslept – they were simply getting lost in their zone. Thembi often causes further frustration on top of this due to her blind and uncontrollable love for food. The team would have barely finished saying the "amen" at the end of grace, and Thembi is already making a dash for the buffet table, muscling her way to the front of the line as possible. She is *that* teammate. The one who shows up last and eats first. Depending on how hungry the players are, her teammates can either find it endearing or excruciating.

The same speed you see me showing on the field? I have that same pace and same look of determination on my face in the dining hall. I employ strategies to try get ahead of my teammates.

On the day of the Spanish game though, Thembi and Jermaine are the first ones in the dining hall. They watch their teammates filter into the room one by one, each wearing a puzzled expression, Janine comes up and puts her hand on Thembi's forehead, pretending to feel her temperature.

"You two are not late... Are you feeling okay?"

The team enjoys a light-hearted yet nervous laugh. Although they are smiling, none can ignore the nagging feeling in the back of their heads that they go into this evening as severe underdogs.

The entire day leading up to an important game is usually meticulously planned. Administrators don't like to give footballers too much time for their minds to wander and play tricks on them. The first thing the team does is pack the bus. According to the rules, that bus cannot be unpacked once the doors have been closed, so players need to make damn sure they have everything they need on them. Next, the coaches take the players through a series of meetings, some of them very technical.

"Thembi, when they go right, that's when you need to switch to your left."

And some of them, purely mental and emotional: "Thembi, be a tiger. Be ruthless. Be vicious. Be fearless. The tiger is nobody's prey."

When the team is in the hotel lobby, waiting to depart for the stadium, they hear a rumble outside. Even though they are a world away, the noise has a tang of familiarity to it. It is a familiar ruckus. It has a distinctive flavour, like the smell of home-made cooking coming through the kitchen window. The noise gets closer and the sounds get clearer. What the players are hearing is voices. The unmistakably deep and haunting echo of a South African war cry washes over the lobby. The players look outside, a hoard of supporters move closer, wrapped in the green and gold pride.

Unashamedly loud on this quiet and conservative French street. The stiff European air is shattered by African song, and it sends a chill down the spine of every Banyana Banyana player sitting in the lobby, "Amahlathi aphelile! Akusekho ukucasha!" (The time to hide in the forest is over! It is time for war!)

The players exit the hotel to greet the delegation. Leading the procession is the South African Minister of Sport, Nathi Mthethwa. He embraces the players warmly and sends reassuring words of comfort and bravery into their minds. Next to the minister stands Mama Joy, a superfan of South African football, whose smile upon victory and tears upon defeat have been a familiar sight in the local game for many years. Her life revolves around showing love to her country, and she has flown all the way across the world to stay true to her cause.

It sounds normal for a delegation from a country to wish their team well before a big tournament, but this is women's football, and support is far from normalised. Many of these players are accustomed to feeling lucky if their family makes the journey out to watch them play.

Now there we were, being greeted by politicians and hordes of supporters. We felt like we were at the centre of the world.

The South African team has long accepted their title as the underdogs of this tournament. They know they will not enjoy the bulk of the support in the stadium, not even close. But after they interact with some of their fans, they realise that they *are* loved. They *are* backed. They *are* supported. The team huddles for a quick meeting before they board the bus, they tell themselves that if there are four people in that stadium supporting South Africa, then those are the four they are playing for. Them and the 60 million people back home.

"We may be far from home, but we are not alone. We carry the nation with us today."

AFTER THE OLYMPICS, BANYANA Banyana gained a certain level of fame in global footballing circles. Partly because they are a solid team that consistently plays above the level expected of them, but also because of the flavour of the team – how they present themselves and how they arrive at the stadium. They are loud. They are unapologetic, and they make sure people know when South Africa is in the building.

On the day of the opening game, as soon as the first player takes her first step onto the bus, the singing begins. The singing never stops. The bus rocks from side to side. No player sits down.

I think it comes from a place deep within our history, printed into our bones, this South African thing of using song to find bravery in impossible moments.

Thembi feels the song deep in her soul. She feels that potent combination of calm and focus wash over her. She sings: "Amahlathi aphelile! Akusekho ukucasha!"

When the bus pulls into the parking lot beneath the stadium, they see the Spanish team bus already there, parked and disembarked. Thembi smiles.

If there is something you don't want, it is to arrive at the stadium before South Africa. You will hear the team coming. You will sit there in the changing room, and you will wait, and you will do nothing as you hear the Africans roar past you. You will wonder who these people are and where we come from.

The Spanish team is doubly unfortunate as South Africa has to pass their changeroom on their way to their own. When Banyana Banyana arrive, only silence seeps through the door of the Europeans. Stamping studs echo off the concrete floor and the players beat a drum line off the dry wall. As they move down the hall, they get louder and louder. They pause for a moment outside the Spanish changeroom, form a circle and sing even louder than before: "Amahlathi aphelile! Akusekho ukucasha!"

The Spanish players try to turn the volume up on their radio, but the Latin American lyrics are easily drowned out by the South African spirit.

The first order of business is always the pitch inspection. Thembi has done thousands of these before, a staple part of the game day routine that she does without even noticing. But today is different. There is something distinct and prestigious about a

World Cup pitch. When Thembi looks at the grass, she sees art. She sees someone with immense pride in their job. Not a blade is out of place, not a lick of paint has spilt somewhere it is not meant to be. The field is symmetrical, pristine, it is alive and it is perfect in Thembi's eyes. She breathes in. She feels the grass. She feels the atmosphere. She nods her head slowly as she looks around. She feels her surname on her back. The letters stick to her shoulders, a subtle reminder that she does not just represent herself today. She feels ready.

Back in the changeroom, the headphones are on, the strapping is tight, the nerves are tangible. Thembi is in the starting line-up. She ties one shoelace. She has barely finished looping it when she has to get up and push past a number of her teammates as she muscles her way to the bathroom. Five minutes later she emerges to tie her other shoe. The doctor keeps an eye on her. When Thembi gets up to sprint to the bathroom again, before finishing her second shoelace, the team doctor is visibly concerned. He raps his knuckles on the bathroom door and asks if everything is okay with her. Thembi calls out, her voice muffled through the bathroom door: "No, don't worry. This is good. This is a really good sign!"

The doctor eases away from the door with hesitant confusion and goes to tend to another player. By the fourth bathroom visit, the rest of the players become concerned, "Hey Kgatlana, are you sick or are you nervous?"

"Neither. I am ready."

The players stand in the tunnel, lined up next to their Spanish foe. There is an intensity about the tunnel; the competitive energy between the two teams is almost too much to be contained in this tight space. It feels as if the whole tunnel may just burst at the seams. The noise from outside does not put the jittery nerves at ease either. The desperate anticipation from the fans outside sounds like hail pelting down on a tin roof, testing the players' bravery, daring them to enter the field. The tunnel only faces one direction though, there is a light at the end of it, and retreating into the darkness is simply not an available option. There have been a few times Thembi has exited this tunnel, and felt herself a different person upon emerging from the darkness, but this time she knows it will be different. She knows whatever lies on the other side of that tunnel will be a world away from anything she has known before.

"Alright, ladies," Janine calls out. "It's time to go."

There is no trace of fear in the captain's voice.

The studs click against the concrete floor as the players shuffle their way out of the tunnel towards their destiny.

Every time South Africa sings the national anthem, the skin on Thembi's arms spooks itself into bumps. She fights back that feeling welling up in her throat. For Thembi, the anthem is a prayer. *Nkosi Sikelel' iAfrika* is haunting. Struggle and sorrow are two threads intimately woven into the fabric of the South African flag. The song is an acknowledgment, a salute to the dark days and those who sacrificed in blood for this nation to be here – it was not easy, to get to a place where Black and white women could stand shoulder to shoulder with a multi-coloured South African flag over their hearts. To be a Black girl in South Africa is to know pain intimately. But the song does not linger in the darkness. It is ultimately a melody of hope. It is a rallying call. A reminder that the odds have never been in the favour of the nation at the tip of Africa. A reminder that no matter what lies ahead, this country has always been through worse – and has overcome it. As the lyrics flow on, Thembi feels the spirit in her blood. She feels her feet, sturdy and strong, standing on the shoulders of the giants who came before her, those who struggled and fought against evil, so that a woman like her might become the hero of her country one day.

"Sounds the call to come together, and united we shall stand. Let us live and strive for freedom, in South Africa, our land."

After the anthems, it is time to shake any emotional distractions that the players may be feeling. Too much emotion allows the situation to overwhelm you, and Thembi knows that she plays best when she is in that zone, when things feel crisp, focused, her thoughts feel sharp, her legs feel light and her soul feels ready.

Thembi drops down to her knees, closes her eyes and points her fingers up to the skies with bent elbows. She uses the moment to have a word with herself: "Thembi, there are people in this world with all the talent but no opportunity. You are lucky in that you have both. There is nothing sadder in this world than wasted talent. So, today, honour yourself with a good performance, honour your team and your fans."

As Thembi comes to the end of her prayer, an international journalist turns around just in time to see the moment, lifts his camera, pulls his focus onto the South African and snaps one of the most striking photographs of this World Cup.

As the game begins, it becomes clear that a big portion of the Spanish game plan involves them marking Thembi out of the game. Every time she gets a sniff of the ball, she finds herself boxed in by two or three bruising Spanish defenders. Thembi cannot speak Spanish (yet), but she recognises her name being badly pronounced over and over as the coach exhausts his voice through huffed Spanish tactical instructions.

Thembi recalls her strategy. She acts overwhelmed at first, like a little girl lost in a market, looking from side to side, unable to see past the big bodies in front of her. She allows the Spanish defenders to dominate her. When they rush her, she does not employ her usual trickery. She can see them relaxing, nodding to each other, acknowledging that their main plan is proving to be effective. As soon as Thembi sees them relax, she comes alive. The way the numbers add up in her head, if there are three defenders on her every time she has the ball, then that means two of her teammates should be free. So she begins to unleash some passes, her opposition numbers are surprised at how quickly Thembi can pull the trigger in such a tight space. Then Thembi does something completely out of character, she hangs back. She spends more time than she should covering her own fullback, ensuring no ball gets through. Confused by the change in heart, the Spanish defence press higher up the field. Thembi feels a smile growing inside. She makes sure not to wear it on her face though. She sees the vast expanse of green grass opening up behind the high-pressing defenders, she looks at it like a blank canvas, and each of her legs a paintbrush, dripping with colour, ready to explode.

After a Spanish set piece, Banyana Banyana find themselves on the counter-attack. Linda moves up the field with the ball, but soon finds herself crowded out by the Spaniards. She looks up the field to see the unmistakable sight of her childhood friend tearing down the wing towards the open space that she has crafted for herself. Linda unleashes the pass. The ball finds Thembi with needle-like accuracy. Thembi controls the ball, making it sit at her feet like a naughty child. Three Spanish defenders form a wall between her and the goal.

You know, growing up eKasi, there are a lot of moves and tricks you learn on that gravel pitch. There is this move we used to do in the township. It was something like a step-over. I'll take you to the right, and then I'll take you to the left. And then by the time I have switched to my right again, you will still be moving left. You will do nothing but watch me move past you, and you will wonder what just happened.

Thembi steps to the right. Thembi steps to the left. She goes right again, and the defender's ankles almost snap off their hinges trying to keep up with the South African.

Thembi uses the outside of her boot and pushes the ball sideways across the edge of the box. The defenders scramble to mark her. They keep their distance though. Thembi is still outside the box, and probably too far out to take an effective shot. In the far corner of Thembi's eye, she sees the unmistakable yellow jersey of one of her teammates. She knows the right and responsible thing to do is pass to her open teammate, giving her the chance to score. But instinct is a funny thing; when placed inside a warrior, it often compels them to go against the safe option.

Thembi does not look up at the goal before she loads her leg back. She opens her shoulders, and then she releases one of the most thunderous shots ever fired by a South African. Thembi feels her shot, but she does not see it. She feels there is something extra about the shot though, a final whip from the end of her boot, sharp and vicious like the sting of a scorpion. Time hangs in the air once the ball leaves Thembi's boot; she waits and she watches. The flight of the ball is poetry in motion; the curve of its trajectory is precise, as if calculated by a science professor. Thembi, her teammates and the whole world watch as the ball sails high, seeming like it is heading for the stands. The keeper runs to cover her corner. She jumps and stretches her finger tips. She has done a good job at covering her goalmouth. This ball fired by Thembi is no normal shot though. It swerves towards the goal, and in its final seconds the ball dips into a tiny space between the keeper's hand and the crossbar. The ball hisses against the back of the goal, creating a beautiful, rolling bulge in the netting. Thembi carries on running, straight to the corner of the field. In the moments leading up to the goal, Thembi noticed an odd silence in the stadium, an unusual calm that seemed to blanket the Le Havre air. Almost as if the thousands of people in the stadium that day knew something that she did not. After Thembi slots the ball into the goal, the place erupts. Her eardrums rattle and distort as the untamed roar resonates out of every corner of the stadium. She chooses to celebrate by placing an open hand next to her ear and extending it forward, asking the crowd, "Where is that silence now? I dare you to not shout."

Linda will remain angry with Thembi for a long time to come following this celebration. Usually, the players rehearse their celebrations in practice, and Thembi's hand to the ear move was nowhere in the training manual. Regardless of this, Thembi's teammates take her lead and just put their hands to their ears too. It is a beautiful sight, 11 South African women lined up to celebrate their country's first-ever World Cup goal. The hand-to-ear gesture is also a salute to their administrators and government officials back home, almost to say – look where we have gotten by ourselves. When will you give the women of our country the professional support they deserve? Can you hear us now?

The Spanish players stare in flabbergasted awe at the space where their keeper once stood. They cannot believe that the small girl from South Africa just plugged one of the classiest goals one could ever see on a football field.

As soon as the final whistle blows, Janine van Wyk jogs over to Thembi, wraps her fingers around the striker's arm and pulls her aside for a quiet word.

"Thembi, how in the hell did you score that goal? I've never seen you take a shot like that."

Thembi looks back behind each shoulder before answering, "Well, you see Janine, I have this theory, but I've never told anyone about it before."

Janine knows Thembi well. She already begins to smile. "And what theory is that?"

"So, you know how I'm a size 4 soccer boot?"

"Yeah."

"Well, this time I asked Nike to send me a size 5."

Janine's eyes widen in disbelief, "But Thembi, why? Did your feet suddenly grow a size?"

"No, no. I still have small feet. But I was up late one night and I was thinking. I reckoned that if there was an inch of air at the front of my boot, that would allow me to get some other kind of vicious whip. I knew it would curl like a frisbee."

"Thembi, you are crazy. Which footballer thinks of wearing a boot one size too big for them?"

"I know I'm crazy, but sometimes crazy works."

The two teammates walk a little further on before the captain stops Thembi and turns to face her.

"Thembi, there is something I have to ask you."

"Shoot."

"There is something I see in your eyes every time you get ready for a game. And I've always wanted to know what you are thinking of when you put on our nation's jersey?"

Thembi smiles. She knows the answer to this question, but it is not one she ever thought she would have to say out loud. She takes a moment to breathe in the stadium atmosphere, absorbing it fully before answering her captain.

'You know, Janine, I create a circle for myself, a circle where I can be my true self, where no one is allowed but me. I know when I put on that Banyana Banyana jersey, I am no longer just Thembi anymore. I am Thembi the footballer, Thembi the role model, Thembi the inspiration. I am Thembi the warrior. When I put on that jersey, I know that I am not just representing myself,

I am representing every African girl child in the world, I am the guardian of her dreams. When I put on that South African jersey, that is me putting on my superhero cape. When I go out onto that field, do you know what I'm thinking about? I'm thinking about the people back home. Our people face thousands of problems every day. There are many people who have lost money, have lost happiness. We come from a place of deep poverty. Some of our people pay what they have and travel thousands of kilometres to come watch us play. Some even walk. For some people, even if it is just one, watching one good game of football can make their week. It is 90 minutes where there are no problems. The problems will still be there after the game, but during the match, it is only football – it is pure. Football is beyond problems. Some may say it is just a game, but many people invest their hearts into this game, so the least that I can do, for my people, for the Black girl child, is to always play my heart out, no matter how difficult the game, no matter how unlikely the odds.'